Vastarien

A Literary Journal

Volume Two, Issue Two

Jon Padgett, Editor-in-Chief

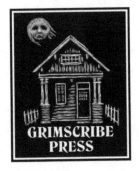

New Orleans, Louisiana

Published by
Grimscribe Press
New Orleans, LA
USA

https://vastarien-journal.com

CONTENTS

ACKNOWLEDGMENTS

Thanks to all our benefactors, particularly James Michael Baker, Chris Cangiano, Iago Faustus, Darren Fisher, Richard D. Hendricks, John LaPre, Adam Rains, Keith Robison, and Robert S. Wilson.

Death & the Maiden
Tatiana Garmendia

Clematis, White and Purple

D. P. Watt

I T WAS early one April evening, at dusk, that I saw another vagrant arrive at the old yard; this one, though, I remembered. I had seen him there at Christmas, I think it was; he had entered through the broken planks of the fence and no doubt found himself some shelter in amongst all the junk that litters the place. I have a good view of it from my dining room—well, I say *good view*. It's really a complete eyesore. I've lost track of the number of times I've written to the council complaining about it, as have many of the neighbors. There's nothing they can do about it, they claim. It is private property—land that they have no responsibility for, or power to order changes to. It would have been a scrapyard at one time. From my window I look down onto it and see the rusting carcasses of old cars; towers of fridges and washing machines, like miniature, snowy mountains; heaps of piping and myriad other useless remnants of yesterday's prized possessions and pristine homes. And there it is now, rotting away in a heap of waste and dust.

It's not just the monstrosity itself that ruins the neighborhood, it's the layers of posters that are plastered on every panel of the fencing that surrounds it; a gaudy palimpsest of last year's concerts and fairgrounds; upcoming valuations of gold and silver and numerous other dubious adverts enticing the reader to 'Earn £1000 a day working from home, call this number' and, naturally, the bright stickers advertising escort agencies and massage parlors. The whole thing looks disgraceful. I'm sure it would affect the price of houses in the area; then again, I'm not moving any time soon. The yard just gets under my skin; how can the owner be allowed to get away with it?

Why I recognized this particular returning tramp I don't know. He seemed no different than the others; the same layers of filthy clothes, even now, with the warmer spring days upon us, a parka done up tightly; the same wrinkled skin, dark from the exposure to the cruel elements; the same battered carrier bags holding his few possessions. I think it was something in the manner in which he entered that I recalled. Most sidled up to the loose planks, gave a few furtive glances to check they weren't being watched, and then crept in. This guy stood before the planks for some time, as though reading the shabby posters intently. Then he bowed his head a moment before reaching out and almost ceremoniously slid aside the loose boards, ducked low through them, as though entering some kind of sacred grotto, and they fell shut behind him like a confessional curtain.

I didn't see him leave. I rarely saw anyone leave. I guess they rose at first light and then went on their way, scavenging and begging. It had seemed to be getting more frequent though, especially in the last couple of weeks; groups of youths would even appear, obviously using the place to take drugs or to drink. Most of the neighbors had noticed too, and I offered to be an informal record-keeper of the increased activity so that we could put further pressure on the authorities to do something about it. I kept a notebook of the comings and goings, with times, and a rough description of each individual and their age. Within a week I had filled one small notebook with information and decided to call the police on Friday evening, when I was sure there were at least eight or nine people in there. About an hour later they arrived, just as it had got dark. They entered, and I saw torch beams flickering about the yard. They were thoroughly covering the whole place but emerged with nobody. They were talking into their walkie talkies as they patrolled the outside fence but then drove off. About an hour later they came back and drove by again, at a crawl. But nobody came out of the yard and nobody else went in. I was frustrated. Clearly, they must have built some hiding place inside, probably underground. If that was the case, then it was getting serious, and we needed something done about it soon. I would go and look around myself the following evening.

Just as I was making ready to explore with a torch, fully charged phone and a small, but heavy hammer (that I could always claim was to repair the fence with, but was more for self-defense), the tramp I had recognized from before appeared again. It had been a sweltering day and the sun was finally setting. But again, he was well covered up in layers with that parka on top of it all. He was without the bags this time though. Perhaps they had been stolen from him by another lowlife. As he approached the entrance, he performed his previous, calm inspection of the posters, followed by carefully drawing back the panels. Then, suddenly, he turned and looked straight up at my house—straight at *me*, it seemed. He stared, holding the panels back with one arm and then slowly—so slowly that it seemed absurd—he beckoned to me, and then went in.

I was unsure how to proceed. It would have been impossible for him to have seen me through the blinds—I keep them at half-tilt when I am watching the yard. Yet he seemed to be looking at me so directly that it was difficult to believe he would be gesturing to someone else. And who would that have been? Mine is the only house that looks directly down the street at the yard, and I would have seen anyone else if they had happened to have been walking by. How on earth could this man know me? How could he have known I had been watching the place? It was ridiculous—I must have misinterpreted his gestures. But I was so jittery I decided to abandon my plans of scouting the place out that evening. Instead I watched as the night came on. I watched for him to leave. He did not. I watched for others that might arrive. Nobody else came. I woke early in the morning to catch him leave, but nobody came out. The whole place was silent and still as the hours crept by, slow hours as I watched and watched and waited and waited.

I went back to bed for a short nap mid-morning, but I could not sleep. I kept thinking of him, his arm reaching out, his hand beckoning me. What could he want from me? It was best to leave the place alone. Perhaps they had got wind that I had called the police, and they didn't want their cozy little drug hovel ruined. I'd best back off for a while, gather more evidence and hope the authorities would finally do something. I needed to take my mind off it and thought I'd take a walk into town to do a few errands.

On my way down the street, I thought I'd take a moment to look at the posters that had so interested my tramp from the previous evening. I stood a good distance away in case he should be watching from behind the panels but close enough to see the posters. They had been hastily daubed up or tacked on with nails—most of the latter had been quite ruined by the weather, just torn fragments remaining. The largest of them was for a visiting circus, one that came every year and that I had seen as a child. A cheerful clown in the bottom left corner pointed up at trapeze artists and other performers in the top right. Bright yellow and orange writing announced,

Markham's Circus, The Greatest Collection of Acrobats and Aerial Artists ever assembled—five days only, 25ᵗʰ-30ᵗʰ May, on The Green by Dock Street, Tickets available from The Box Office at Pallas Hall, Call Now!

There was nothing particularly remarkable about it. Even though it was clearly a recent addition, what struck me as odd was the direction to obtain tickets from Pallas Hall, the council office that had closed down a few years ago. I remembered some argument in the local paper about it and protests. It had been sold to developers to turn into flats, along with other, older council buildings in the town. All of the council services had then been brought together and moved out of town to some bland modern building. I would have to check on it when I returned home. Perhaps I was wrong.

The next one that had taken his interest was slightly smaller but just as gaudy and attention grabbing: two men stared face to face at each other only a few inches apart. One was dressed in a dark costume with a black mask on that only allowed a small slit for his eyes. The other was muscular and heavily tanned, his torso oiled and bulging. The text of the poster ran down the gap between them and read,

Announcing the return of The Dark Ninja, terror of terrors, for one last grudge match against The Dancing Bear – Max Logan. One Night. One Match. One Winner. 14th April. Mather's Arena. www.darkninjadancingbear.com

The date had passed so no doubt this would get covered over soon enough by another one. The other few nearby were much smaller, and I needed to move closer to read them. A small, A4-sized one, without an image, simply read,

Car Boot Sale, St Michaels Church Car Park, every Sunday 10-4pm (stalls from 8am), Come and grab a bargain!

Another, of similar size, had an image of a professional looking woman in glasses looking at a clipboard, a small text in a functional font read,

Ever thought about looking into your credit history? Someone else has! For independent financial advice and recommendations for future investment opportunities give the Finance Specialists a call! Open 24/7, on UK-based lines, to arrange an appointment.

The only other one in the vicinity that the tramp might also have looked at was smaller, with a picture of a fine-looking country house on it,

Bathurst Hall and Garden. A fun day out for all the family.

Take a tour of the stately home from April to October, seeing

the collections of fine paintings and sculpture acquired by the

first Baron Bathurst and visit the Orangery in full majesty!

Ample Car Parking and plenty to entertain the children!

I had visited Bathurst Hall a few years previously as a treat for my mother a couple of months before she passed away. I had found the place rather disappointing and overpriced. There was little to do there really, and mother was too unwell to take advantage of the lovely garden. We had sat a long while in the warmth of the Orangery in silence.

I stepped back and viewed the posters together. Quite what he had seen in them was beyond me. Whatever convergence, or message, had captivated him must have been more the product of his disturbed, or drug-addled, mind than anything apparent to a sane person.

As I was about to go, I noticed the top of the fencing was covered in tendrils of climbing plants, small creepers with their spidery stems reached over, seeking to spread themselves beyond the confines of the tatty yard. I had not really noticed any greenery in there from the vantage point of my house. Peering a little closer, it appeared to be honeysuckle – better than dreaded knot or bindweed, I thought.

In town, I concluded my business fairly quickly, but the ridiculous, aggressive expressions of The Night Ninja and Max Logan – The Dancing Bear kept plaguing me. What a silly thing wrestling was, I thought—a ludicrous sport more suited to the gullibility of children.

Fitting that it should be displayed beside a circus poster, both flashy entertainments. I saw the same posters in a number of places around the town—strange how such things effect a brief, performative change on a town and then vanish.

Down by the train station I saw something else that disturbed me in a rather different manner. It was a missing person poster. *Emily Wardle, 20 years old, left her home in Hedham for a night out in Manchester by train, did not return. Not seen since 7th April 2018. If you have seen Emily or know her whereabouts, please contact the Police immediately on 999.* There was a photograph of the woman, clearly taken for a passport; stern and focused. I knew Emily, although I had not seen her in nearly ten years. I used to teach piano for a little extra cash and had become friends with her father at the cricket club. He mentioned her love of music, and so I'd offered some discounted lessons. She was a nice girl, quiet and very studious. She practiced her playing regularly but there was no real skill or, indeed, passion for it. I think she had felt obliged to pretend to like it, either for her parents or to acquire something that might have set her apart from the other children in some fashion. The last I'd heard of her she'd gone away to university in London to study politics.

I pondered the sadness of a lost young person. What had happened to her? What terrible things had she been caught up in? There might have been a perfectly reasonable explanation; perhaps the family hid a history of abuse and she was breaking away to make a new life for herself; perhaps she had dark secrets of her own misdeeds she wanted to remain hidden. The possibilities were endless—sadly, I thought, it was (as is often the case in these circumstances) unlikely she would be found.

It was at that very moment, sunk in dark thoughts about a dark world, that I chanced to encounter Peter McIntyre. We'd played together in a band many years before—just covers and wedding gigs, nothing special—and then worked on some cruise ships before parting ways about ten years previously. We'd always got on well and shared many an enjoyable evening. Apparently, he'd married a woman from Bahrain, and they'd had two children. Now they were divorced, and he was back home and had set up as an agent, of all things! We had a lot to catch up on and went for a drink. A few drinks later, we went for a curry. After a long evening of too much wine and pleasurable company, I found myself tottering home, wishing I'd ordered a taxi.

Coming back onto my road, making ready for the steeper climb to home, I glanced along at the wretched wall of the old scrapyard, with its ludicrous posters and disintegrating fencing. Someone had tried to remove some of the posters earlier that day, at least, especially around the loose planks. Perhaps they were finally going to do something, were perhaps going to repair the fencing in an attempt to sell the land. I drunkenly ambled over to the cleared area and then heard a scramble of feet from the yard beyond. Foolishly emboldened, I decided to stick my head in and see what was going on.

What I saw was quite incredible. Amongst the rusty, old crap there were countless wildflowers and climbing plants that wreathed themselves around the rusty poles and disintegrating cars. The yellow light of the streetlamp cast an odd glow over the curious scene; there was something profound about it—the reclamation of our detritus by the power of nature. No doubt it was the emotional flush of the alcohol in me, but I felt connected to the space in a way that was as surprising as it was deep. I was with it enough to realize that venturing further in—to a disused space where drug addicts and vagrants congregated—would be crazy, and I ducked back out and turned to home.

Then a word on the fencing caught my eye. It was a tattered scrap left from one of the posters—*Green*. Having just seen the transformation of the yard beyond and the flowers, it struck me as quite appropriate; one of those lovely moments of synchronicity. I staggered back a little, and gave out a hiccup that made me giggle like a child—I had not been this tipsy in some time. There were other words that sprang from the scraped poster shards:

Greatest

Green

at

Dark   of

Night

Come

into

the

Garden

It took a moment to sink in, and then I muttered,

Greatest Green
at
Dark of
Night
Come
into

the
Garden

It was a stupid thing to have bothered with, just old fragments from last month's adverts. I was disappointed in myself. I headed up to the house and put the kettle on; I needed some coffee. But the words, the place... *the green garden*... the flowers. Surely there was some kind of meaning in it. It kept running on and on in my head, *Greatest green at dark of night. Come into the garden.* I ditched the coffee and poured a half tumbler of brandy, even though my head was still pounding from all the drinking earlier with Peter. I went over to the blinds and peered through them at the yard. The streetlights illuminated the poster remnants, swaying in the breeze like little flags, and some of the mounds of decaying junk, but I couldn't see any of the greenery—with the abundance I had seen in there I should certainly have a good view of it from here.

Then a figure appeared and walked with purpose towards the yard's hidden entrance. She was slight to the point of being worryingly thin, with drainpipe black jeans and a well-worn leather jacket. She paused a moment, pulled the planks aside and backed in, just as the tramp had done. Just before she disappeared into the darkness, she looked up, and the streetlight caught her face fully.

It was Emily Wardle.

I dropped the glass.

She looked straight at me, just as the tramp had, and then—as my heart began to pound with terror—she beckoned to me. I pulled the blinds. I breathed heavily and thought I might pass out. I sat down and waited a few minutes, trying to control my panic.

When I had composed myself, I opened the blinds again. The

street was empty. The planks were closed. A cat loped across the road and then ran beneath a parked car, pursuing some unseen prey. I watched a while for further light in the yard. Nothing.

I decided to head down there again and grabbed my torch and phone.

The yard was even more transformed than it had been that short while before. It was no longer a pile of rusting junk, intertwined with beautiful flowers and creeping plants, it had become a resplendent garden in full bloom—great, tall gladioli sprouted their stems of magnificent bells up to chest height from everywhere; every kind of hyacinth crammed the few discernible pathways through the undergrowth, and the whole ground was carpeted in soft mosses and chamomile, the latter giving off its sweet scent with every footstep I took into the wonderland; for truly it was wonderous. I gazed in awe, like a child in Santa's grotto, marveling at the trailing vines that hung overhead, rich with fruit. Through them were twined great coiled branches of wisteria, its delicate lilac petals falling in brief flurries as I passed beneath—Adam in Eden.

I came to the heart of the yard, where a trickle of a steam ran into a shallow pool that reflected the dark sky and bright moon. All about me was a kind of blue luminescence that seemed to have no discernible source. It gave everything a ghostly hue, but I was not afraid. The whole place was tranquil, restful, welcoming. Around the edges of the pool some sort of structure had been raised, through which climbed numerous clematis. They were obviously very old, having knotted themselves into a dense bower under which I could look up and see the great open blooms, their long feathery petals like quills, reaching out to caress me, the large clusters of their stamens like fragile spidery legs twitching in the cool breeze. I stroked the length of one of the petals, from the heart of the flower to the tip. It was a dark purple in the center, gently fading to white at the edges. It was soft as young skin, and I could have stood there for hours, just stroking the flowers and gazing in awe at the exquisiteness about me. But I heard a great sigh and came to my senses quickly.

"Emily," I called, softly. "Is that you, Emily?"

"Yesssss…" came a drawn-out, breathless voice.

It was coming from a great wall of clematis that had grown up against what might have been a heap of old tyres. I gently moved aside some of the flowers from where I had heard the voice.

There was Emily, or the *new Emily*, her pale skin bright in the odd light, her eyes ringed with dark circles from sleepless nights and anxious days. From her nose, mouth and ears there coiled thin, bright green creepers that grew steadily even as I looked on in amazement. Thin lines of blood trailed down her cheeks; her eyes stared upwards into the night in agony and awe.

"Enjoy the beauty of the night garden…" she whispered.

I was not scared; I was numb with shock. There was something terrifying about the terrible tendrils that threaded through her but also something damningly beautiful. There was a rapture to her smile. The thicker creepers held her bound to the wall of tyres behind her—but, wait, they were not tyres. It was a wall of skulls in different stages of decomposition, some older ones, near the base, were a clean creamy color, without any flesh, fused together with thick, trunk-like creepers; further up one could make out matted tufts of hair—blond, black and brown—and festering clumps of flesh; the occasional glutinous eyeball that looked like a shriveled slug. It was a wall of rot that was growing through poor Emily Wardle. As I looked at the gruesome scene, I caught a glimpse of a green coat beside her, further into the tangle of stems and flowers. I pulled them aside. It was what remained of the tramp I had seen, his clothes protruded here and there, a hand, its twisted fingers twined with creepers. Little remained of his face, the mouth choked with greenery, leaves protruding from his nostrils and a huge flower blooming from his right eye. Again, I was less horrified than overwhelmed.

I breathed deeply, trying to compose myself to determine what I should do next. But the whole, grotesque scene was intoxicating, with gorgeous fragrances of roses and buddleia, lilacs and lilies—in the background there were notes of jasmine and rosemary, mint and lavender. It was as though the whole garden had become a perfume, seducing me, drawing me into its lavish luxury.

I dropped my torch, I had no need of it, other senses led me on, and besides the moon was bright, and more fitting to illuminate this splendid hell. I wandered on in an appalled stupor and realized that it was not heaps of rusting cars and fridges that abounded throughout the yard but piles of rotting corpses, some bloated with flies, others corpulent with bacteria, ripe to burst, fertilizing the ground with bounteous ordure. The piles of pipes were bones as plenteous as any charnel house might hold. And through, beneath, above and between everything there were the flowers of every color and size, all clamoring for the attention of the insects that busied themselves about the place, even in the dead of night—everything was collapsing into a discourse of substances: blood and water, flesh and nectar.

Reaching the perimeter of the yard, I came to another labyrinth of clematis and honeysuckle, from which protruded a femur or humerus here, a rib or jawbone there. I laughed and stroked the white and purple petals of the flowers as I had before. I leaned against them, embraced them, welcomed them to me.

We do not want to *be* with you, here in The Night Garden, we want to be *beside* you. We are things adjacent; we are brothers, but we are not kin. We are the invisible reaching out of an eager young stem, we are the twisted trails of snails and slugs and the gathering of dew on early morning grass. We are the dim light in the owl's eyes and the rich traces that fill the badger's snout. We are the padding of a fox's paws on wet tarmac and the shimmer of a weasel through the undergrowth. We need you to whisper worms into your dead flesh, so that they can tell us what it is to be a body when they rise again, transformed on filthy wings. We need you to sew with magnificent blooms of fungi and mold, so that their rotten colors can show us the truth of being present. We need to whistle the winter wind through your dry bones so the music can dance us into the solidity of reality—for a moment, just a moment. For here in The Night Garden, where we have dwelt forever, everything is fantasy—everything is blank and white with possibility, awaiting the savagery of creation. Your bloated remains are the purple canvas upon which we read the artistry of existence and draw you into the void of eternity. All is silver and mist here in The Night Garden; our promises are the chill of night air; we are your last breath and final dream.

Silence Continues
Danielle Hark

like crickets

Robin Gow

there is a chorus of meal worms
a strange amber writhing
a toad will close its eyes
to swallow
a room full of crickets
leaping over each other
& asking louder & louder
if the grass has changed
colors while they've been away
all the insects in the pet store
are waiting to be eaten
aren't they?
they have to know on
some level what their
crowding means & when
i am in a crowded subway car

this is all i can think about
how we look like crickets
legs thin & jutting
eyes posed wide &
unable to blink
click-clack of the train
moving there are reptile
shadows all moving too smooth
a graffiti born predator
i go to the pet store
& i sit in front of cages
of prey & i tell them they
need to find a way out
they need to leave now
before they're
taken & set in terrariums
with hungry animals
who have to close their eyes
to swallow
i never close my eyes when
i'm eating as a precaution
the lights all go out
in the subway car & i consider
becoming a cricket down there
in the damp & the cool
the lights all come on
& the people are all meal worms
everyone of them around my ankles
like soft bracelets
it's me then it's me
i'm the reptile moving
gentle as water
a tongue scooping insects

i get on my crooked knees
& eat them
eat all the people
who had been in the subway car
with me
& i get out & tell no one
what i've accomplished
& run to the pet store
to warn the crickets
& the meal worms
to get out while they
can get out of the city
& go live with family
in tall grass somewhere
tell stories about how close
your bodies were together
leg crossing leg
fingers eyes antennae
twitching with crowd

not other's tongues

Robin Gow

who hasn't eaten
their whole tongue before
while they were asleep?
that night hunger
that demands swallowing
it grows back
of course but slowly
i open my mouth
in the mirror
a blank room
all those back rows
of teeth i'm not
used to seeing
little off white rocks

as if there's a shoreline
i didn't know about
in the back of my throat
i think about cow tongues
in the case at the butcher shop
& fields full of cows
without their tongues
they open their mouths
to each other as if to ask
the other cows if
someone is really eating
their tongues tonight
i eat my own tongue
not other's tongues
though one time i was
kissing a boy & he bit
my tongue which i thought
was strange & for a moment
i wondered what that would
be like to feed someone else
a piece of my body
if, he might, like a dog
scarf the limb down
if the blood would pool
in my mouth
yes that's where the ocean
would come in
the blood would just
go out into the ocean
spilling over the teeth-rocks
he didn't of course
he just bit the tongue
i'm the one eating here

& i'll spend today
checking my mouth
& waiting for the tongue
to start re-growing
a tiny little
tongue-bulb pushing
up from the soil bottom
of my mouth
drink water
whisper kindnesses
to the tongue
i tell the tongue
i'm sorry for what
i do in my sleep
but that in our sleeps
we're not really responsible
for what we do
that's someone else
who sleeps for us
& conjures our strange dreams
of tongues moving
across the ground
like fat worms
i give the tongue
sunshine & open my mouth
to the back window where
the beams sneak in
i tell the tongue
i'll try not to do it again
& my yard fills up with cows
all without tongues
come to warn my tongue
not to grow back

i tell the cows to hush
i tell the cows i need
a tongue
even though i know i'll
bite it off again
its body falling
perpetually past the rocks
& into the ocean

types of knife blades:

Robin Gow

serrated, santoku,
boning, bird's beak, paring
fingernail, fire wood,
the swing set that buried itself,
the smell of cold rain
sharpening itself into my shoes,
a bottle cap, a falling of bottle caps
from somewhere high up, the moon
visible in the afternoon, hair ties,
a light switch blinking
back/forth, a wrong pillowcase
a strand of jupiter color hair,
your tongue across my chest—
slicing me open: beautiful fish,
guppies, sardines, school bells
somewhere all metal, sirens

chirping/ pretending to be birds,
birds—all the birds— all their beaks
opening/ cutting craft paper,
the cruelness of April,
saying "i want to die" but really
just wanting to dissolve,
saying "i want to live" but
really just out of curiosity
about how many colors pleated skin
can make in the aftermath
of a knife— more for the list
syringe, thank yous, refrigerator,
falling asleep, forget everything,
a ripe staircase, a righteous lamp,
the floor of someone else's bedroom
where you pressed me down—
all the scars on my back,
all the scars on my chest,
all the emptiness of the word
scar because you think it's
metaphorical, needing a better
word for "scar" : fissure, cleft,
breach, ravine, rift, rupture—
a bracelet swallowed, a finger
tracing across your chin—
look at me severing you—
we sharpen each other's knives
with our bodies— the way skin
in a greedy surface, the way skin
is asking to aperture,
the way the floor is
a type of knife
and so are we

The Stringer of Wiltsburg Farm

Eden Royce

DADDY CALLED TOBACCO a quick and dirty crop. Quick because it was one hundred days from planting to harvest. Dirty because cutting the leaves released a juicy, dark sap that clung, sticky sweet, to the skin. Mud then stuck to the sap, eventually drying to a thick crust that itched and flaked, turning my brown skin ghost gray.

Didn't keep him from sending me out in the fields.

"It's 1949," I told him, tying an apron over my dungarees. I poured coffee from the percolator. "Times are changing."

Daddy hobbled to the kitchen table, leaning his weight on his horn-head cane. He spat a thick wad of chaw into an old ashtray and my stomach turned at the yeasty smell. Tarry juice stuck to his beard and he wiped it away with his arm.

"Not dat much, Annie Maggie. Not 'round here." He glanced

at the sun coming up over the trees, drying the dew on the crop. "Still got cuttin' and pullin' ta do."

I shuddered. I knew which job was mine. One of the blades from a used harvesting machine Daddy bought from some white man upstate had come lose and torn a gash in his leg from knee to ankle. Until that healed, he couldn't be in his own fields like he wanted, cutting and pulling, chewing and spitting, alongside his farm hands. Back bent to the tasks, sweat pouring off him like it was coming out of a bucket. Smiling all the while.

"I still have school."

"You had plenny of schooling, gal. More'n ya mamma or me ever had."

"I know." I put a cast iron pan on the stove and tried to keep the disappointment out of my mouth. They'd worked hard to get me here: almost eighteen with a few more months until I could get myself a diploma, then take the county test to be a teacher myself. But that would have to wait. Daddy was hurt, Mamma was dead, and Jeannie had gone and gotten married.

My sister married the first man showed any interest in her. She hated this farm. Said the smell of drying leaves and manure made her retch. Daddy heard her one time and waxed her tail good for talking mess about what put food on the table and clothes on her back. Jeannie never said anything else about the farm out loud, but it was in her eyes every day—the hatred she was choking back. Smart and pretty as she was, she grabbed onto the first raggedy boy going somewhere out of town and held on for dear life.

Her letters came every so often about her hand embroidery and the homemade peach and fig jams she sold at the corner market. But she never visited. One of the ladies from church went to visit her aunt up there in Neville and said she heard Jeannie yelling at her husband for smoking a cigarette. Told me my sister said she wouldn't be in no house with no man that smoked. Kicked up such a fuss, he stomped out the offending stick and grabbed Jeannie's arm and dragged her home.

That left Daddy and me to handle everything in those hundred days. We hired croppers for the cutting, usually three or four men. Including Daddy, it was barely enough to get the leaves to market on time.

I stared out at the fields, not really seeing the sun come up and stain the sky. The fatback in the pan sizzled and popped, stinging my arm with a drop of hot grease. I winced, took the pan off the stove eye.

Daddy slurped a mouthful of coffee. "I don' know why you won' marry one a dese men and have some chirren can help us 'round here. They's good workers, each and ev'ry one."

"Hm."

"What wrong wit 'em? You ackin' like dey t'baccy man or somethin'."

I snorted as I lifted the crisp bacon from the pan and drained it on a towel. The tobacco man was a silly story that croppers told to keep owners from having them out in the fields at night. *Betta crop while the sun shines, or t'baccy man gon' git you. He come and cover you wit da'kness – den you gone.*

Never did find out where the tobacco man was supposed to take his victims. If he was out there, maybe I should go and ask him if he's seen Mamma. I busied myself and had eggs, scrambled hard, and day-old buttered biscuits with the bacon. We ate in silence, Daddy knowing I didn't like talking about marriage and kids, but he did it anyway. Always thinking about what was best for the farm.

I didn't want babies. No one I had to be responsible for. Each time I said it, he got this look of pity on his face, and told me I'd change my mind. Women were changeable, he'd said. I'd learn. I'd be a good mother.

But I'd seen how Mamma declined in the hours after her baby boy came out stillborn. She hollered and cried, wailed long, throat-drying warbles until grief turned her into a banshee, and she flew off into the night.

Daddy never talked about that night. After the baby came out cold and blue-brown, he cursed, then pushed up from the bed and grabbed a bottle of white lightnin'. On his way downstairs, he told Jeannie and me to clean Mamma up. Jeannie poured hot water from the kettle into a basin and grabbed some washrags. I pinned Mamma's sweaty hair back and whispered to her, but she didn't speak, didn't move, while we carefully washed and dressed her. When we went to wash the baby, she started to cry.

Daddy came back upstairs then. His eyes were shiny-bright under the lamplight as he followed Mamma's hollering. Loud, choking, gasping sobs, like she wouldn't ever stop. Jeannie and I clung to her, but she swayed like curtains on a clothesline—no substance left to her at all. Daddy told us to move, but we didn't until he shouted at us. We'd scurried to the opposite corner of the room to wait and watch.

He'd held onto Mamma's shaking body, clad in the floral cotton nightgown we put on her, as she screamed her pain. Soon, she started fading, getting thinner and lighter until we could see the whitewashed walls through her deep brown skin. Jeannie and I could only stare, unable to move, as Daddy clutched at her, his big, rough hands tangling in her pressed hair and tearing her nightclothes. Soon his hands fell free all on their own and Mamma's ghostly body slipped through the keyhole in the front door.

We all ran to the door and threw it open, calling her to come back, but she was gone, the inky, starless night swallowing any trace of her. Tobacco leaves waved in the breeze, a half-hearted good-bye. The next day, on my walk to school, I found a dusty, dirt-flecked piece of that flowered cotton beside the fields and put it in my bag.

Now, some eight years later, I'd sewn it into a quilt I kept on my bed. When I missed her too much I climbed under that quilt. Rubbed that scrap of faded cloth, and imagined Mamma not as a monster, but finally having freedom and peace. Even though it meant my ties to this place only got tighter.

I put our empty dishes in the sink as Daddy took a drink of medicine from the amber bottle a root doctor gave him. He'd never been fond of hospitals. They tended to turn Negroes away, so he kept his ailments close to his chest and called on local healers when he couldn't stand anymore.

As I took off my apron and put on my boots—an old pair of Daddy's—he asked, "You goin' stringing when the men get here?"

I nodded. He wasn't going to spend money to hire a woman to tie up the bundles of cut leaves when I had two good hands and a strong back. "Gotta pick first, though. Then I'll feed the chickens."

Daddy grunted, the medicine already taking effect. I checked the bandages on his mauled leg before he shuffled to the worn sofa. "You's a good girl, Annie Maggie."

I picked up the tin bucket next to the door.

"Yeah," I mumbled. "Too good."

The day was blister hot. The chickens warbled and clucked

while they scooted around my feet, angling for the best position to get the most feed. I tossed out a small handful of corn from my pocket.

"You'll have to wait for the rest, ladies. And gentleman." The banty rooster stared at me with one unblinking eye, then tilted his head away as though he had better things to ogle.

I marched out to the furthest row from the house, my stomach bucking at the job ahead. Maybe the large breakfast hadn't been a good idea, as it threatened to come back up. I sucked in deep breaths through my mouth to calm the churning, sure that, if I vomited, I'd only feel worse when the birds flocked down to feed on it.

Peering close to the tobacco plant, I reached out and grabbed a fat cutworm, then pulled it from the leaf. It wriggled in my grasp, its multitude of legs waving as it roiled. A deep brown stain of tobacco sap showed where the creature's mouth was. My gut lurched. I dropped the creature into the bucket and moved to the next one, hoping I was out early enough to mitigate the damage of the worms' feast.

Left alone, these cutworms—fat-bodied caterpillars with stumpy legs and an endless appetite—could destroy a crop in less than half the time it took to harvest. They had to be removed by hand. Pesticides were no good. They killed every other bug, but these hardy worms were immune and continued to glut themselves on the soft leaves.

Daddy usually pulled, his wide fingers the same thickness as the bright green worms. He would grab three or four in succession, before dropping them all into the bucket. He said he couldn't feel them struggling against the callouses on his hands.

I felt them wriggling against my palm, trying to squirm through my fingers. One of them bit my hand, right where the thumb and first finger meet. The pain was at first a pinch, then it blossomed into a stabbing that shot up my arm to my heart. I let loose a curse, yanking off the offender and mashing it in my fingers. I threw the mush in the dirt, ground it under my heel until it disappeared.

I sucked on the wound, the metal-sharp taste of my blood strong. Out here in the middle of the ripening leaves, I could only hear the symphony of thousands of mouths chewing, devouring. Moist snapping, followed by the musky, oily scent of wet tobacco, and manure-rich dirt. Times like this, I understood Jeannie more than I'd ever say.

I pressed my lips together and went back to my task, pulling off the destructive cutworms, their softness hitting the bottom of the tin bucket with a sick clunk. I kept on until the clunk became a gentle plop, the worms' plump bodies cushioning the fall of their brothers. Soon, they'd wriggle to the lip of the bucket and out, determined to feed.

One cropper named Ray Earl told me the worms get addicted to the tobacco. That was when I first started helping Daddy in the fields, as a young girl. Right when Mamma got pregnant with that last child.

"Them worms get to where they won't eat nothin' else. They does anything for that weed."

Back then, he was about the age I am now, barrel-broad in the chest with legs that looked too skinny to hold him upright. He slipped a piece of cut cane between his lips and sucked. "Dat's why you neber gon' see me wit' it."

And I didn't. Every evening, most croppers sat on the porch with a piece of leaf from the day's cuttings. They were filthy, covered in dark sap dusted over with mud and muck, but they sat wiping spittle from their chins and yakking away until dusk, their chewing loud as the worms.

Ray Earl would get his pay, thank Daddy kindly, then head off to wherever it was he lived. He'd be back the next morning, ready to work. He was the one who first told me about tobacco man.

I laughed to myself as I pulled more worms. I'd believed every word Ray Earl had said. Looking up at him, seeing his rough hands darkened even further by the clinging sap, and edged with a line of powdery ashiness on the knuckles, fascinated me.

Know why you 'posed to wait 'til sunup to start with t'baccy?

I shook my head, fat pigtails smacking my round cheeks.

'Cause that's when t'baccy man sleep. Don' want him catchin' you.

I'd screamed a little, and he turned serious eyes on me. *Don' worry, Annuh Magguh. I aine gon' let him git you.*

I think I'd been a little in love with him then. But he must've gotten killed in the war, because he never came back after that harvest. I'd forgotten about him and his story. Strange how things come back.

The bucket was about a third full. I hefted it after wrapping a dishtowel around the handle to protect my hands. After so little time in the fields recently, my hands had gotten soft, unused to the labor of harvesting.

I trudged back to the house, leaning to balance the extra weight. Some worms tried to crawl out, but I shook the bucket, so they tumbled back down to await their fate.

In the yard, the chickens swarmed me, *tuck-tuck-tucking* the food call to each other. I sprinkled the worms in a narrow line through the middle of the brood. The birds pounced, scrabbling for the bloated worms, their toenails scratching the work leather on my boots as they rushed to glut themselves.

One of the birds, a frizzle hen, was scratching in another part of the yard. I shooed the black-feathered bird away, and knelt to look at what it had uncovered. A red felt bag tied with coarse twine—a mojo hand. I backed away, almost dropping the bucket. I was no root lady, but I knew magic working when I saw it.

I peeked inside to ask Daddy, but he was snoring on the sofa, fast asleep from the pain medicine. I saw some of the workers coming toward the house, the younger boys who came with their daddies to work the crops, their slim fingers pinching off the tobacco flowers as they began to grow. One light brown boy bent over the water pump in the yard, getting a drink, and I called to him.

"Young man," I asked. "You know where Dr. Beetle lives?"

He looked at me with a frown, his pouty little mouth dripping water. "Dat root man? Yeah, I know."

Of course he did. Conjure healers were the only medicine we had, except for the granny remedies to cure everyday ailments: sick stomachs, heatstroke, women's heavy monthlies. Rootworkers created salves and poultices for cuts and scrapes, boiled leaves into tonic—it was big business. One thing croppers didn't have to worry about was flies and mosquitoes. Insects couldn't abide the smell of the sap.

"Please get him for me," I said, reaching into my pocket to hand him a coin and a piece of peanut candy I'd made, wrapped in waxed paper. "Tell him I found something."

The boy looked at me while he unwrapped the candy. He popped the square into his mouth, then turned and took off, running for all he was worth through the dirt and empty wooden poles standing upright in the fields.

I trudged to the nearest one in my borrowed boots, pulling a roll of string from my pocket. I tied together the stacks of leaves the cutters

35

had left, then hung them on the poles for the wagon to gather, keeping an eye out for Dr. Beetle's arrival.

The short, thin man chuckled when he saw the mojo hand. "This what your hen scratch up, eh? Who you trying to get?"

I never messed with magic. I was going to school so I wouldn't have to live my life worrying about who was laying tricks on me or hexing my family. Teaching was a suitable job, and I'd send money to Daddy whenever I could, but these fields full of their caterpillar worms and black sap-coated superstition weren't for me.

"It's a protection mojo. Nothing wrong with a little help now and then." He looked up at me through his blue-lensed sunglasses and adjusted his hat to shade his eyes. "You could use some help, ain't that so?"

"No, thank you. Daddy will be up and around soon, and things'll go back to normal. All we have to do is get through this harvest and sale. We'll be all right."

"No shame in asking for help, young lady."

I bristled, but held my poise. "You're right. When I need help, I'll surely ask for it. I called you here today, didn't I?"

Dr. Beetle folded his frail arms across his bird-like chest. He looked directly in my face for long moments, making me uncomfortable with seeing my reflection in the blue lenses. "That you did. You getting along, then?"

"We're managing all right."

He ran his tongue, pink as trout flesh, over his bottom lip. "Uh huh. How's Jesse?"

"Daddy's fine. You can go see him if you like. He's inside."

With a nod, the doctor shoved his hands in his pockets and headed for the house.

"What do I do with this thing?" I pointed to the dusty, worn pouch in the dirt. The chickens were giving it a wide berth.

Halfway in the door, he turned back. "Bury it right back where it was."

I frowned. "Why? Nobody here needs protecting."

"Now how would you know that, Annie Maggie?" He stepped the rest of the way in the house and shut the door.

I picked up the bag with a sturdy chicken feather, carried it to the drying shed and dumped it in the fire.

That night, I dreamed a wet mouth met mine in the dark as slick flesh slid across my body. I rose to meet it, pressing deeper into the tender recesses. It was like no other kiss I'd had—not from any of the croppers, not from the other girls at school who liked to pretend they were kissing each other to practice for when a boy wanted them. This kiss was a feast, a feeding.

I fell into a nothingness made of tongues and mouths. I could see nothing, only feel smooth, roiling skin under my fingers. I heard my breath and another's, huffing bursts of heat into the chilled night. I tasted sticky-sweet smoke, felt the tiny, welcome pain as teeth nipped at my lips.

I tugged on the skin, tough as fabric in my hands, wanting to be closer, to feel this swirling madness, this ache pulsing low in me. From a distance, I heard my name whispered, then louder and louder until it rang out, breaking the daze I was in. I sat up in the middle of the fields, shuddered at the cool dew seeping through my nightgown. Lights went on in the house upstairs, first one, then a long time later another. Daddy was moving around on his own, calling for me.

"Annie Maggie!" Daddy's voice rose with his fear of not finding me.

When I put my hands to the ground, leaves clung to my palms. I yanked them off, jumped to my feet and raced for the house. I made as little noise as possible getting in, unsure how I'd ended up outside. We kept a mirror on the wall right inside the door to stop ghosts entering. As I passed, I caught a glimpse of my reflection.

My hair was wild, loosened from the braid I wore it in to sleep. But what made a cry wedge in my throat was the dark brown stain covering my mouth. I touched it with my dirt-covered fingers, wincing as they made contact. They came away coated in cedar-red, the color of blood and sap. My lips stung.

Daddy let loose a string of curses when he saw me. "Answer me when I calls you, girl. You think you's too old for me to whip, but…"

His voice died when I faced him. I trembled as a sound like a wail from behind a pressing hand escaped. Him or me, I wasn't sure.

Eyes round as moons, Daddy backed away, hitting his leg against the buffet table, hard. He didn't flinch, not even as fresh blood began to seep through the previously white bandage. Not until I started toward him.

He held his walking cane out to stop me.

"What you been out in them fields doin', girl?" As I tried to stammer a reply, he slammed the cane down on the hardwood floor, and I jumped at the sound of cracking wood. "Don't play wit me, girl! You know good and damn well what I'm talking 'bout."

I tried to smooth out the snarls in my hair, my quivering hands making the tumble of straight and coiled strands worse. I drew the damp sleeve of my nightgown over my mouth.

Daddy's eyes were shining, full of held-in tears. He turned his head up to the ceiling, and trails of water ran down his cheeks. The lamp in the hallway distorted his shadow into something hideous.

"No, no, no!" he shouted. "I lost Marie to that thing, and I damn sure ain't gonna lose my child to it."

I didn't know if his words were for me or for himself or for God, and I didn't care. "What about Mamma?"

He jumped as if he'd forgotten I was there. His lips quivered. "He took…he took her."

"No, Daddy. She left that night cause the wailing called her, and she had to go." I tried to pick at the grime under my nails, but it wouldn't move. "The grief was too much because she wanted a boy baby so bad."

Daddy shook his head. Tears flowed freely down his brown face, leaving streaks of salt white.

"No, what?"

He babbled. 'Mercy' and 'Jesus' were the only words I could make out.

"You might as well tell me." I stepped forward, but he backed away down the hallway toward the stairs. I pursued, knowing I looked like Mamma did when she left and not caring. Not anymore. "Tell me, Daddy! About Mamma—what happened?"

"You was only a child. You and yo' sister."

His side hit the wall, and he curled into it, sliding down the plaster to thud into a sitting position on the floor. A smear of blood from the soaked bandage stained the whitewash.

Fury burned the back of my throat, filling it with the taste of smoke and ash. My voice pitched up, shaking the framed pictures of Jeannie and me on the hall table. "Now, Daddy!"

"She couldn't have no boy child. Just you girls. I wouldn't let her rest until she had one."

The taste of tobacco sap coated my mouth, sweet and smoke green, familiar as a lover's kiss. My stomach growled.

His words came thick and fast, trying to explain, to get me to see. "If she couldn't have a boy I tol' her... I tol' her she could find somewheres else to go."

All I saw was a haze of cedar red. Blood and sap.

I swept the pictures from the table, glass shattering at my bare feet. "I thought you loved her!" My scream shook the boards of the house. From far away, I heard a familiar wail, full of lonely fury.

Daddy seemed to rally at that, losing some of the fear that had crept into his face. "I loved her! It was her that step out on me!"

"What?"

"After she gone that night, I looked good at that boy baby. Ain't look nothing like me." He spat the words out like a plug of chew that had lost its flavor. "Looked same as that ol' cropper thought he was too good to stay 'round after meals."

"Roy Earl?"

The bottom dropped out of my stomach, the taste of bile and green tobacco bubbling to fill it. I stepped forward again, shards of glass biting deep into my bare feet. Daddy's shadow grew ink black, spread further along the wall.

He come and cover you wit da'kness —

Den you gone.

"Yeah, yeah. I found him that next evenin' and I showed him that boy, told him I knew… I knew what he was doing with my wife." Brownish spittle dribbled from his chin, but he didn't bother to wipe it away. His shadow flickered and rose behind him.

"I put both that boy child and his pappy in the ground that night—out there in the middle of them fields." He sneered. "Both of 'em."

I watched the shadow pull away from the wall, wave like a flag in a breeze. It folded over Daddy's shoulder, then down his arm, curling toward his waist. The smell of the tobacco leaves grew, weeping out from that dimness.

"That's why I set that mojo hand. Protect you and your sister from me." His leg wept openly now, the red blood darkening to a syrupy brown. "It held good for a while."

"Dear God," I whispered. The memory of slick, roiling worm flesh against my own, teeth nipping at my lips, brought back familiar words, the image of dark knuckles white with ash.

Don' worry, Annuh Magguh.

I aine gon' let him git you.

Daddy's eyes rolled, whites stark against his skin. His words were back to a babble as the shadow cloaked him in smoky darkness. "Best for the leaves. Best for the farm."

"Stop."

"Boys stay. Girls leave. Boys…"

"Stop it, Daddy."

"Best boys. Need a boy for the farm." His shadow swam over his good leg, his bad one, traveled toward his face. "Boys best boys. Girls don't—"

41

"Shut up!" I screamed, the wail opening my mouth larger than should be possible. Cutworms poured from my lips, plopping and plunking down to the hardwood floor, their segmented bodies writhing and rolling to right themselves. My scream cut through the still night, waking the chickens, who joined my wail with their insistent fear-ridden cackle.

The worms swarmed toward my daddy, crawling over each other in a desperate attempt to reach him, mouths already working, chewing. Leaves rustled, wet with dew and something denser that dropped to the floor in fat plops.

Daddy shuddered, but didn't try to get away. He knew what had come for him. My throat was dry, raw, and still I hollered. The worms fell faster, more than I'd ever seen in my life. They reached the tobacco-scented shadow covering Daddy and they tore at it, chewing… always hungry. Always chewing.

I saw through my transparent skin to the swarm of bright green creatures on the floorboard, gnawing. Another wail came from across the fields, and the sound of Mamma's voice brought tears to my eyes.

My cry went on until my throat burned and all the fight left me. I fell against the banister to the second floor, panting. I held onto it as I walked upstairs to my room, avoiding the crush of writhing cutworms feeding on their favorite meal.

Filthy, sticky with dirt and sap, I slept.

When I came down the next morning, washed and dressed, with my bags packed, Daddy didn't ask where I was going. He just looked at me, diminished from his usual upright stance and nodded.

"Bye, Daddy." I hefted the quilt further under my arm, carried my burdens down the front steps and across the fields, to the bus stop that would take me into town.

I didn't look back.

I learned he died a few years later, and I returned to the farm to make his homegoing arrangements. Jeannie said she had a husband and three kids to look after, but she would do her best to attend. I had his body cremated, and sprinkled his ashes over the tobacco fields he loved more than anything. Or anyone.

For the last time, I strung up the stacks of tobacco leaves. I paid off Daddy's bank loan with the proceeds from the sale of that final harvest. There was some money left, and I made sure all the croppers got a bit extra in their pockets. The farm itself and all the equipment, I sold before returning to my little shotgun home and my own classroom of kids.

Jeannie never made it back to help me tie up the loose ends, but she happily took the check I offered.

Fragmented
Danielle Hark

The Pelt

Christi Nogle

W HEN MY HUSBAND first bought me the mansion, I'll
admit I was lost for a time. I slept hard on the sofa and
woke coated in sour sweat. My belly bloated and
rumbled, then drove me ravenous to the phone to order something
meaty. When my feet got sticky, I ordered rugs. I didn't think of
cleaning but of buying things to cover the filth, and in my deeper
mind I was trying to work out what more I could buy so that the
house would be a home and reasonable and tasteful, so that everyone
else could see how I loved it and why. That's the space I was in, poor
soul!

When my husband bought me the mansion. I know how it sounds, but this house was cheap, cheap, cheap because the hill view burned away. The real estate agent said it would be back to green in a year or two, but she and I and my husband laughed and laughed when she said that. I remember we stood in some back part of the house that looked out through all of the front porches and all of the back porches and somehow also gave a view the stairs, a white-tiled space smelling of lavender and mildew and echoing with our manic laughter, which gave it all a slipping, circling carousel feel.

The neighbors who could afford to do so moved after the burn. The ones who couldn't afford to, older couples, they stayed inside growing ever more bitter about the loss as the new people trickled in, large families that started with sectionals and wide curved TVs and just kept bringing more and more mobster-looking furniture from Costco and having grinning brown boxes delivered. *They* didn't need a view because they had all the wonderland inside, I suppose.

But no, a house like this one *doesn't* need a view. It's miles away the best on the street (I know, never buy the best one on the street— but that's if you're thinking of money). This house would be something even if it were parked next to a smoke-belching factory or a pig facility—but here, here there's just no view and the lawns are little bit brown, or really, more of a gray. It's all kind of gray outside, whatever the weather, come to think of it. But that's all that's wrong.

Well, why did your husband buy you a mansion? When he came into a little money, I thought he'd want to spend it on Europe, but it turned out he wanted to spend it getting me out on my own. Who could blame him? I was a mess.

I remember all the feelings swelling inside me when we sat in the truck after he said yes, that I could have it—just a thrill of feeling, so loud. I saw him speaking but didn't catch his words.

"Claire? What did I say?" he said.

"Furniture the house," I said. What an odd way of putting it, like to "people" something. I knew it must be how one said it, but it didn't sound right.

"Within reason, that's the important part. I will pay to *furnish* this house. Within reason."

The doorbell? I wrestled my way up from the sinking couch, unlocked the first door and the second door and the third. Gray light hit me hard.

A barrel-bellied man on the step said, "Delivery."

Out in the street idled a flatbed truck with an enormous roll of something on it—a roll like carpet but too thick and bouncy to be carpet. Beyond the truck, neighbors brought their heads out of their cargo areas to look at me.

A roll of something springy like pancake appeared in the street, but they stared past it to *me* because they never see me.

"Wrong house," I said, but the man beckoned me out, pointed to numbers on the house and numbers on the sheet. He said they matched, and I couldn't argue.

The truck was already backed in, young workmen already unrolling the roll. I did have a dim recollection of ordering a red, fluffy bathmat and flat, green kitchen rug. The phone screen was so small, though, and my eyes were getting old.

The color hit me, a red like orange and pink and brown—so much color, so loud. The workmen were still unrolling it and kept unrolling. I caught that the fur lightened at the tips like split ends. The pelt, then, of an Elmo who'd lived too hard and had too many home perms. I still thought it was a rug.

"It's awfully . . . Max and Betty," I said, and when the man was blank, I said. "I mean lurid, tacky. It'll have to go back."

"You think?" said the barrel man.

I was outside for the first time in who knows when. I even came off the step to pull up on the edge of this thing. It was so light I thought again of pancake, five or six inches thick with the base a whorl of fibers and dry white clay flaking off of them. And seeds. Small black seeds stuck to my palm. A young man took my corner from me and guided me away so his partner could get it nailed to the ground. Two more men were still unrolling the other end. It was going to span the entire yard.

"I can't have this," I said. It was definitely Max and Betty, and more importantly, it was not what I'd ordered, or maybe it was, and I'd failed to take down the dimensions. Or I didn't deserve something like this—maybe that's what I thought. Whatever. It was wrong.

But the red carpet was over the grass now—it *was* the grass— and the young men were getting back in the truck.

"It looks great, so eco-friendly too. Good choice," said the barrel man. He put a rough hand on my shoulder and lingered on his next words. I knew someone had told him to say it: "It gives the place a real *autumnal* feel."

It was the right word. That thing cast a light that made me feel cool and wakeful for a change. Like fall, like going back to school—the promise of industry, something occult at the back of it.

The man's face was close and smiling, all dark stubbled like a cartoon husband. All of a sudden, I wanted him to come inside.

"For a minute," I said, touched his shoulder. He backed away. Before it was over, we had some hard words.

My husband had done this to me, or he had done this for me. I remembered it both ways and was not sure which was true or if either was. Each memory was also a projection into the future, like this:

Possibility number one: one year in the future, I will be tan and positively gristling with muscle in a black sheath holding a glass of wine in Europe. My hair will feather better than it has ever feathered. I won't hate wine anymore. I'll love it, even though I still don't know nearly as much about it as my husband does. Someone asks about me, and my first impulse is to say I was lost for a time, but my husband pulls close and begins the story of my renovation project and how in fact the view did re-green ahead of schedule, and I made some lofty connections through blogging about my heroic renovation and became some kind of fabulous interior designer or remodeler or whatever.

The past for this future is an excited conversation we had in the truck after our first tour of the house.

Possibility number two: one year in the future, I am still sleeping on this sofa.

The past for this future is me hyperventilating, crying snot into the sofa the moment his truck backed out of the driveway.

Your husband's truck or the barrel-bellied delivery driver's truck? Both.

Anyone could see which story was true. And I had lied to myself when I thought I remembered some thrill of feeling. I didn't remember feeling.

Five to seven-bedroom suites unfolded somewhere upstairs, extra bedrooms needed in case my daughters came. When Mary came, though, I stood inside the door of the first porch and said anything I could to make her leave. All the time I was thinking it was not possible I had once been so overcome with feeling to disobey my parents and take all the other harrowing steps to make her, have her, keep her. I wasn't that person.

My husband didn't set me free hoping I'd come back stronger; he threw me away because he couldn't suffer my hatred and lethargy anymore. (I heard his mocking voice, "Oh the world is ending! Oh!") It was true I'd been in a low rage over things I wouldn't or couldn't change. I wouldn't make any move, so he moved me.

What was the inside of the house like? I'm not picturing it. Tall white rooms with complicated windows and fireplaces, rooms smelling of plaster and mice, more rooms peopled with ghosts. Ghosts of Christmas parties past and future, dinner parties, school projects done at the table, so much baking and rushing around before work, painting and cleaning and furnishing. Rooms furnitured with vague and see-through wardrobes, carved and scrolled in gone gray wood.

Rooms furnitured with canopied beds and tapestries and cities of silver-edged photographs on console tables that were not there.

The sound of it all drove me to the drawing room or parlor or whatever. The morning room? The front room, anyway, right inside the porches where I had my sofa. The ghosts kept me there trapped and static, a little bug in amber.

But with the arrival of all that autumnal red, I decided that memories and pre-living were what had kept me on the sofa. From that time on, I resolved to live in the moment.

I stood before the first porch looking through the second porch and third to the neighbor's houses beyond and the lawn, a red rectangle one hundred feet wide by seventy-five deep. . .

No, the measurements are remnants too of the past. They're not what I'm seeing. I'm seeing the red line of the lawn.

No, I do not see a red line. I see white verticals overlapping thinner gray verticals, overlapping thinner darker verticals—that's what the porches come to from this angle. White squares and rectangles up high for the sky, a mess of gray shapes for neighbors' bushes and lawns and the street, red rectangles lower down for the beautiful new pelt. I isolate one of the shapes and look at it alone—a square of sunset cloud. Very satisfying.

I looked and looked, who knew how long? I felt some little thrill or thought I did.

That night I had my first dream of the house. It was a stupid dream, all told. Instead of three porches, there were endless porches and me racing to lock all of the French doors on each of them because some big terrible thing was coming. I hurried up the stairway, which went on longer than any stairway could, and then the steps became vestigial steps that smoothed to nothing so that I climbed a steep ramp that became a complete vertical, and I clawed and gnawed at the carpet until I crested onto the landing. Someone waited for me back in a softly lit bedroom, asked sleepily if I'd locked the doors.

When I woke, I cried—just briefly, but I cried because he wasn't there.

And on a sunny afternoon when Audrey brought her baby, I didn't stand inside the door. I went out the back and came around, so she'd think I'd been working outside. I didn't cast a glance toward the pool on my way.

I greeted her warmly as I could. We sat cross-legged, and she admired how the lawn cast pink light over the porches, balconies, and turrets so that, even though the clapboard siding was patched in many shades of white and gray, and flaking, and powdery dry, it looked carved of pink stone like a princess house in a dream.

The baby grasped the lawn in his fists and made big eyes at us. Audrey laughed and said, "He's like, 'This is a thing?' "

I wiped his silky drool into the fibers and felt something.

The rains come at night. I lay on the sofa imagining ponds in the lawn fur, shatters of gold and brown leaves, mud—in short, a big mess I won't have the energy to clean—but it isn't like that in the morning. The lawn feels soft and dry when I touch it gingerly, like wet paint can feel dry when you're gentle. When I pad across barefoot, I squish down deep. I leave pink footprints on the porch boards.

The rains do not stop soon. The street goes grayer than ever before with a low dark ceiling overhead. I simply watch from the step and do not think or judge. Silver light comes and then white. A pink rainbow appears. Neighbors come back from work eager for their mail. They shuffle it before their faces and do not bother to look in my direction. My skin dries and warms and finally begins to feel vexed, and up from the carpet come pale cordyceps mushrooms, little segmented vines with spiked flowerbuds, soft little worms.

When the air cools at night, it's just enough to freeze around the ghosts in the swimming pool. I can't keep myself from standing at the edge to see the shards of ice build around their channels. A man and a woman, I think, swimming precise laps. The edges of the channels go slushy, and if I bend down close, I can sometimes see the shape of an elbow or of splayed fingers pushing out into the slurry of water and ice and dirt and leaves—yes, the first autumn leaves!

Standing by the pool gives me a good crisp feeling that turns to chill as soon as I turn my back, but I can't help going out there. My feet stay cold for hours afterward, and I promise myself I will not go again.

When Ava and the boys come, I can't keep them away from the pool. It's afternoon, no chance of them seeing anything, but still I feel protective when, in the course of our picking leaves out of the fibers in front, we move closer and closer to the side gate and the tallest boy, the one with pumpkin-colored hair, peers over and says, "No way."

The boys aren't all ours. One or two are friends, neighbor boys, and one are two are Ava's, but I can't say which. As we circle the edge, they say they could clean it, for pay of course, and then they say even for free. They argue amongst themselves about whether to consider cleaning it for free, then they whine in unison to be allowed. And if they could be allowed to clean it, they could be over here all the time swimming, and I would not have to be so lonely, they say.

Ava wanders off when it's clear I will not budge on this. The pool stays as it is. It will not be cleaned, will not be drained. If it freezes and cracks, just as well. Two more of the boys follow after her, but one stays.

He comes close. "Your house is what you have when you're old, isn't it? It's how you get other old people to come over and think you're cool."

I'm struck how much he looks like my husband then, the features just the same but more perfect, more smug if that's possible.

"I wasn't always as popular as I am now," he says. Something in his voice tells me he feels very noble just now. He lays a hand on my back, would lay it on my shoulder if it reached. Leaves rustle all around, and the cool dusty smell of autumn swirls around in my hair.

"I used to be *un*popular, actually, but then I made one good friend who had the . . . courage to be real with me and tell me what I needed to do."

Bright white teeth barely show out the corners of a thin sneer.

"Would you like me to be honest with you?" he says, but just then the Ava calls out. She and the other boys are approaching the gray SUV parked on the street. They're far away, tiny, faceless.

"Would you?" he says.

I look down. The ground is thick with leaves now, orange and pink and brown and glossy yellow. Graying grass pokes through in some places still, but the truth is that, even here in the back, the ruddy pelt has made inroads. The thatches sticking out between the leaves are as likely as not to be pink.

When the green kitchen rug came, the kitchen was so distant. I placed the return label on the package and set it back in the mailbox.

I will furnish *the house within reason,* he'd said, but I had no reasonable needs. Did you know, for example, that you can dry off the rain just as well with a wash towel as with a bath towel? It doesn't get any wetter than the bath towel would get.

What I came with was more than enough: my phone, my sofa, a suitcase of clothes, a basket piled with washcloths and cosmetics. He'd offered things from his garage and basement in case I needed time to decide on a scheme, but I'd refused. I had little enough use for anything except the phone and the beloved sofa that still sat in front of the fireplace where he'd left it, a curvy cut-velvet thing that was my bed and chair and table (my protector, my fort, my cave). It was the right piece for a mansion, the spills and gloss of sweat and even the sunken springs being a bit gothic somehow and not out of place. Its pattern read as paisley or coleus leaves, and though its threads had many colors, from a distance it read as red as the pelt beyond the doors.

That time I dreamed of the doors and climbing the stairs that became the ramp, when I came to the top and my husband asked whether I'd locked the doors, that wasn't the end of the dream. I'd doubted myself and turned back—down a different staircase, of course—to check the doors, which turned out to be an arduous task because to check the outer ones I had to unlock layer on layer of inner ones and then check each layer in order. An arduous task, but I finished and, blood pulsing in my head, set off to find the back staircase and finally get upstairs to sleep. I caught, though, a tuft of red just inside the first porch. I unlocked the door, and the draft blew the thing off to the right into shadow. I followed, and of course I found a gap in the wall, unfinished rooms leading off the porch and more rooms beyond those filled with filth and the sounds and smells of distant rain, and finally, at the end of the stupid labyrinth, a wall missing and the water barreling down on red, red grass.

So, there was no way to lock the house after all, and whatever horrible thing that would come would come. Great terror and gasping! In the dream, I think I was a caricature of myself before all of this, striving and stress-driven, always afraid of what's outside.

I don't have that kind of dread any longer, and it turns out that one needs a little dread to make a home. A little dread, a little projecting into the future and into memory. Without it, one cannot imagine which furnishings or which tasteful wall coverings are needed, one can't desire to recreate tender moments with the kin, or anything like that. A kitchen's built on dread. A luxurious bathroom—are you kidding?—absolute dread.

I wonder, does your husband notice there are no charges on his cards except your food deliveries? That is what you're saying, unless we're wrong. You've done nothing to furnish the house. You've done nothing, all this time.

Maybe he's so flush he hasn't been looking at statements? Sure, or charging so much of his own that he thinks it's both of ours. I decided some time ago to stop wondering.

I spend more time outside now, sleep less. My waking is as relaxing and restorative as sleep. I've depended on the sofa so much for so long now and loved it in my way. I decide to set it free soon. I will drag it beyond the lawn for someone to take—but no, the time to think about that will be when I'm dragging it, not now. The time to think about food will be when the delivery car comes, not now.

For now, I lay back in the sumptuous pile admiring rows of black trunks still stuck like nails into the burned hill, the fallen ones like Roman numerals here and there. Birds go over. Every one of them, even the occasional black one, is red breasted by the glow.

I think of times my husband drove past a yard with too many seasonal decorations, or with a cardboard cutout of an old woman leaning over to weed, or a tire painted white with flowers inside, a gnome or birdbath—even a birdbath—he'd say "That's real Max and Betty" after the neighbors who lived across the street when he was a boy. They took joy in garden kitsch and for that they'd been a joke with him all of his life.

If he drove past *this* house—and who knows? Maybe he does drive past. Of course, he does—it's what he says. I know it. I can decide to stop knowing it, though, so I do.

I think that if I could open the house to the street, if I could unfold it to show what's inside, the neighbors would surely come to help. They'd bring their castoff things and all their hoarded cheer. Casseroles.

As the house is now, still enfolded, anything could be behind the porches. I wonder what they imagine inside and then decide to stop wondering. It works. I decide whatever I want, and it's so.

I roll onto my belly so I can run my fingers through the grass. A spiky fungus catches at a hangnail, and I flick it off. The flowers do not bloom here. In fact, their buds have disappeared. Their tough little stems make U-turns back down. I can see them growing through the grass to the grid layer and through the clayey fibers of the base, through dead lawn through soil through gravel. They shuttle through concrete and wood and burst into bloom in a forgotten cellar far below, where no one but I can see them.

Silences

Lucy A. Snyder

The newborn won't cry
not even after the surgery
to remove its rotting twin.
Unmade parents lying awake,
3am, exhausted in the dark.
The father's quiet dressing,
slipping out into the cold grey
dawn, destination unknown,
too dazed to make a hard turn.
The soft November snowfall
blanketing the overturned car.
Fifteen frantic texts unseen,
muted in a red-soaked coat.

Thomas Ligotti
Giuseppe Balestra

Visions of the Gothic Body in Thomas Ligotti's Short Stories[1]

Deborah Bridle

Although Ligotti is not a Gothic writer strictly speaking, he still proposes to his readers an array of creatures that variously range on the scale of monstrosity. Those creatures, however far they may roam from the Gothic vampires and ghosts, correspond nonetheless to the definition that Maurice Lévy put forward in his paper "Aspects du corps gothique : histoire, discours et fantasme:" "the Gothic is the Other, of course, but it might be more accurate to say it is *the body of*

---

[1] This paper is a translation of my paper entitled "Visions du corps gothique dans les nouvelles de Thomas Ligotti". It was written after my participation to a conference organised at the Université de Bordeaux Montaigne in 2015 in tribute to two French scholars, Maurice Lévy and Jacques Goimard – "Théories et esthétiques des genres de l'imaginaire : autour des travaux de Maurice Lévy et Jacques Goimard".

the Other."[2] The Other is obviously the monster, that which is identified above all by its alterity and its difference, that which we do not want to be: "the monster is a by-product of our hallucinatory and desperate desire to posit humanity as a unique thing."[3] Therefore, it matters little that Ligotti takes us far beyond Radcliffe's sublime landscapes and terrifying dungeons, since the Gothic body is an ever-changing construction. Indeed, as Lévy explains in his analysis of the changes experienced by the Gothic body through the 19th century due to the scientific discoveries of the time, the Gothic body is defined by "its profound instability, . . . its absolute alterity, and . . . its dependence on the cultural discourse of its time."[4]

This paper seeks to question the status of the Gothic body in the work of Thomas Ligotti based on the "cultural discourse" that accompanied its creation. As textual objects, Ligotti's bodies are bodies that are displayed, monsters in the etymological sense of the word, even though one would prefer to keep them hidden in the dark. I will therefore first establish a typology of the Gothic bodies that can be found in Ligotti's stories based on Lévy's analysis in "Aspects du

---

[2] Maurice Lévy, "Aspects du corps gothique : histoire, discours et fantasme," in *Les représentations du corps dans les œuvres fantastiques et de science-fiction : figures et fantasmes*, ed. Françoise Dupeyron-Lafay (Paris: Michel Houdiard éditeur, 2006), 72. All quotations from Maurice Lévy and Jacques Goimard are translated by me (apart from quotations from Lévy's *Lovecraft, a Study in the Fantastic*: translation by S. T. Joshi).

[3] Jacques Goimard, *Critique du fantastique et de l'insolite* (Paris: Pocket, 2003), 279-280.

[4] Maurice Lévy, "Aspects du corps gothique : histoire, discours et fantasme," in *Les représentations du corps dans les œuvres fantastiques et de science-fiction : figures et fantasmes*, ed. Françoise Dupeyron-Lafay (Paris: Michel Houdiard éditeur, 2006), 81.

corps gothique," before studying the function of those bodies inside the author's work and thought. From an aesthetics of the fantastic, how does the Ligottian body manage to serve a metaphysical vision, namely a representation of the absurdity of reality? How does that vision illustrate the "unity of the abyss," a concept that Lévy borrows from Bachelard to describe "the materialisation of a somewhat metaphysical void that the act of writing seeks to mask"?[5]

I. Catalogue of a Gothic hybridity

In "Aspects du corps gothique," Lévy explains that the Gothic novel has rendered possible the concrete and physical representation of the human body's functions heretofore silenced – or addressed from a moral or a philosophical perspective – like sexuality, suffering, and death. Even what is left unspoken in Radcliffe's works implicitly suggests things like a real feminine sexual desire. With the triumph of science in the 19th century, the fantastic genre became the locus of all the fantasies and fears associated with the body: the theory of evolution gave birth to visions of degenerative bodies and the Gothic "toys with this hypothetical instability of the body that science puts forward."[6] In the second half of the century, the fantastic text was contaminated by instances of metamorphosis, transformation, vampirisation, backwards evolution. What the first age of the Gothic left unsaid gave way to an all-too-clear representation of those

---

[5] Maurice Lévy, "Approches du Texte Fantastique," *Caliban* 16 (1979): 15.

[6] Maurice Lévy, "Aspects du corps gothique : histoire, discours et fantasme," in *Les représentations du corps dans les œuvres fantastiques et de science-fiction : figures et fantasmes*, ed. Françoise Dupeyron-Lafay (Paris: Michel Houdiard éditeur, 2006), 78.

mutating bodies: "the Gothic is the return to the invertebrate. The monster leaves its metaphorical status and achieves materialisation."[7]

Even though the "cultural discourse" mentioned earlier has necessarily changed since the scientific discoveries of the Victorian era, the monstrous body has nonetheless kept its privileged place in horror literature ever since. Lovecraft's hybrid gods as well as the mutations undergone by some of his characters illustrate that tendency. The monstrous is still effective because it offers such rich and diverse variations that its literary and symbolic treatment is inexhaustible. In *Lovecraft, a Study in the Fantastic*, Lévy notes that the fantastic monster emerged at the beginning of the 19th century but that the one imagined by Lovecraft has tremendously distanced itself from its ancestors:

> But although in the Romantic era, fond as it was of excess, the monstrous was only too often the rusty machinery of horror, there is at the source of the extraordinary creatures invented by Lovecraft a dynamism of imagination, which gives them a profound and redoubtable originality.[8]

The composite aspect of those monsters is not simply the result of a fortuitous assemblage but of a process of hybridisation and contamination, two phenomena that are also at the core of Ligotti's representation of the body. Let us note, first, that, as in Lovecraft, the body in Ligotti's works is not presented in its sexual function.[9] Bodies

---

[7] Ibid., 76.

[8] Maurice Lévy, *Lovecraft, a Study in the Fantastic*, trans. S. T. Joshi (Detroit: Wayne State University Press, 1988), 56.

[9] One might object by citing the episode from *My Work is Not Yet Done*, when Mary's body, turned into a mannequin, is sexually violated by two vagabonds, but I argue that this scene belongs to the horrific more than it does the sexual.

are represented in their monstrous dimension, but this dimension comes to the readers and the characters under many guises, varying in shape and purpose. It would not do justice to Ligotti to reduce his bodies to mere hybrids: establishing a typology of those bodies would help us better understand their function in the Ligottian corpus and their resonance in the author's thought.

When presented in its entirety, the body in Ligotti rarely comes out unscathed in the story – it might be marked by the stigmata of monstrosity from the start or be modified in the course of the plot. The motif of transformation, dear to the fantastic, enables us to establish a classification based on the opposition between the static and the dynamic. Three categories thus emerge: fragmentation (when the integrity of human body as indivisible whole is compromised), hybridity (when the body is represented as a composite whole from the start), and contamination (when the body undergoes transformation in the course of the story). This typology is also a way to consider the notion of liminality. Indeed, Matt Cardin underlines Ligotti's use of a subject's decentring and quotes on the matter structuralist Edmund Leach: "whenever we make category distinctions within a unified field . . . it is the boundaries that matter: we concentrate our attention on the differences, not the similarities, and this makes us feel that the markers of such boundaries are of special value, 'sacred', 'taboo'."[10]

Puppets and mannequins being favorite objects for Ligotti, it is not surprising to see that many stories feature broken human bodies, not unlike dismantled dolls. Fragmentation can occur within a

---

[10] Matt Cardin, "Liminal Terror and Collective Identity in Thomas Ligotti's 'The Shadow at the Bottom of the World'," in *The Thomas Ligotti Reader*, ed. Darrell Schweitzer (Holicong: Wildside Press, 2003), 88.

seemingly intact body. In "In a Foreign Town, in a Foreign Land," the narrator does not immediately notice anything about Mrs. Pyk, the owner of the hotel where he has rented a room. But his eyes are soon drawn to her hands. The first is paralysed ("a thin and palsied hand"[11]), while the second – first represented through its difference from the other one ("Mrs. Pyk's left hand, the non-palsied hand"[12]) – is afflicted by another form of alterity since it is an artificial hand that the narrator compares right away to that of a mannequin whose flaky paint replaces skin. From this moment on, the woman's hands keep resurfacing every time the narrator describes her, showing his obsession with them. In "The Last Feast of Harlequin," the strange people that the narrator meets in a café are broken apart, reduced to body parts that seem to emerge from the indistinct mass they form, from the vacant eyes that look around the place to the heap of legs that seek to trip the narrator ("Unseen legs became entangled with my own"[13]). The author also goes beyond those symbolic fragmentations and actually breaks bodies apart. Parts and pieces of dolls and mannequins are scattered around Dr. Voke's loft ("Dr. Voke and Mr. Veech"), a mysterious factory manufactures a series of weird objects, some of them looking like body parts ("a peculiar ashen lump that betrayed some semblance of a face or clawing fingers" in "The Red Tower"[14]) while others are presented like replicas of human organs or appendices such as hands whose fingernails grow during the night and eyeballs set in lumps of lava. Interestingly, both the human and the

---

[11] Thomas Ligotti, *Teatro Grottesco* (London: Virgin Books Ltd, 2008), 128.
[12] Ibid.
[13] Thomas Ligotti, *Songs of a Dead Dreamer and Grimscribe* (New York: Penguin Books, 2015), 275.
[14] Thomas Ligotti, *Teatro Grottesco* (London: Virgin Books Ltd, 2008), 67.

artificial bodies can be subjected to the same fragmentation process. The collapse of boundaries between human and object reinforces the horror. The mannequin legs emptied of their stuffing and scattered around Dr. Voke's loft are just as terrifying as the body of the woman that he has preserved, because their difference only hangs by a tenuous thread which threatens to break at any moment.

In my second category – hybridity – that thread has effectively been broken. Hybridity is a meaning-loaded term, one that Lévy and many other critics tie in to the fears that Darwin helped uncover and for which the fantastic is a very fertile mode of expression. As mentioned above, hybridity takes on many forms with Ligotti: all categories are prone to change, all species are porous. In "In a Foreign Town, in a Foreign Land," Ligotti describes a macabre procession in which all sorts of objects are attached to the bars of a cage set atop a cart, offering the reader an enumeration that heralds the possibility of all fusions. The animal, the inanimate, the dead, the artificial, and the human are all on the same level: "I saw masks and shoes, household utensils and naked dolls, large bleached bones and the skeletons of small animals, bottles of colored glass, the head of a dog with a rusty chain wrapped several times around its neck."[15]

One of Ligotti's most fruitful blends is that of the living and the object. We can find it in the objects made in the strange factory in "The Red Tower:" other than the creations mentioned above and among many examples, the manufacture produces a music box whose melody has been replaced by a death rattle and a watch whose hands are tiny insects and reptilian tongues.

Hybridising objects and living beings is notably achieved in the figure of the mannequin. The terms "mannikin" and "puppet" are

---

[15] Ibid., 140.

recurrently used by Ligotti, both in a literal and in a figurative sense. In "The Clown Puppet," the narrator regularly makes a strange encounter with a human-sized puppet whose strings are manipulated by an invisible hand, each encounter weirder than the one before. Other than those images of living puppets, Ligotti also describes objectified humans who look like puppets – a very frequent metaphor in the author's stories, as the few following examples show: "now he appeared to be no more than a malignant puppet of madness,"[16] "he spied vague silhouettes that moved hectically in a bright window, twisting and leaning upon the glass like shadow-puppets in the fever of some mad dispute,"[17] "Beneath it was a limp-limbed effigy, a collapsed puppet sprawled upon the slab."[18] The puppet metaphor enables the author to describe the loss of humanity, no matter how that humanity supposedly defines who we are as humans, while leaving a doubt regarding the metaphor itself: is it really only valid on a symbolic level?

The disincarnation of the human body is often explored and used by Ligotti, not only by hybridising human and object, but also through a fusion between the categories of the human, the botanical, and/or the animal. In the story "Les Fleurs," the narrator has made a strange sculpture that is at a crossroads between art, flora, and fauna, with leaves armed with teeth and a body covered with something akin to fur. A similar imagery is developed in "Flowers of the Abyss," in which the botanical seems to merge with several different elements – the arms of one character are compared to branches while the flowers in the garden, which are the central focus of the story, look like hellish

---

[16] Ibid., 208.
[17] Ibid., 236.
[18] Ibid., 290.

creatures ready to devour anyone who would get too close: "these things squirmed, a wormy mass that was trying to make itself part of me," "a convulsing tangle of shapes, like the radiant entrails of hell," "creaturely forms strung with sticky and pumping veins, hung with working mouths," "slimy tendrils."[19] Architecture, a Gothic element *par excellence*, receives the same treatment as the house is first compared to a blooming plant, then to a poisonous mushroom. Places are often described as organic locations in Ligotti's work, as they become in turn hybrid entities, at the same time inanimate spaces and living bodies. The whole story "The Glamour" revolves around a mysterious cinema which gets more and more similar to the interior of a human body in which lights emit a red or purple glow reminding the narrator of arteries or a heart, and whose pink walls are not unlike the convolutions of a brain. "Nethescurial" offers the same spatial hybridity: this Lovecraftian story features a manuscript telling about the existence of a cult which worships an evil and primordial god. The island where the members of the cult would gather is scattered with warts and tumours in the shape of hills and trees, and the stones are covered with moss compared to leprosy.[20] The idol resting on the cult's altar is characterised by its absolute hybridity, a mixture of human, animal, vegetal, and inanimate elements: "these outlines which alluded to both man and beast, flower and insect, reptiles, stones, and countless things I could not even name, all seemed to be changing, mingling in a thousand ways that prevented any sensible image of the idol."[21]

---

[19] Ibid., 316-317.
[20] Ibid., 321.
[21] Ibid., 328.

This dynamic vision of hybridity leads to my third category: contamination. Lévy often highlights in *Lovecraft* the author's obsession with degeneration, something that he and other critics have linked to Lovecraft's racism. There is none of Lovecraft's questionable position in Ligotti's work, and yet a veritable kinship exists between their visions of contamination and corruption. According to Lévy, "the monster is revolting not only because it escapes logic and constitutes a disturbance for the reason, but also because it is propagated and, little by little, corrupts the individuals of a healthy race. In a land of fantasy no one can be certain – and the reader least of all – that he will not someday be changed into a monster."[22] The principle of contamination and danger is associated to a seemingly irrational monstrosity which deepens its terrifying dimension. None of Ligotti's characters is safe from suddenly finding themselves at the core of some process of monstrous mutation. The porous limits of hybridisation are further weakened when bodies leave their supposedly unalterable status and find themselves in the margins. Contamination highlights this in-between space of liminality. In "The Chymist," the pharmacologist is not simply trying to transform a prostitute using the drugs he is developing: he is attempting to recreate her, to make her a specimen of a brand new species beyond the human or the floral, a creature transcending those limits, as hinted by his bloodcurdling words at the end of the story: "The consequence of this is simple – you can never be as you once were. I'm very sorry. You'll have to remain in whatever curious incarnation you take on at the dream's end. Which should rattle the wits of whoever is

---

[22] Maurice Lévy, *Lovecraft, a Study in the Fantastic*, trans. S. T. Joshi (Detroit: Wayne State University Press, 1988), 57.

unfortunate enough to find you . . . Now Rose of madness –
BLOOM!"[23]

Contamination can also infect a human and make them shift to
the animal. In "The Sect of the Idiot," the narrator, while dreaming,
meets a group of strange beings, all members of a sect. Under their
cloaks and hoods, it is easy to perceive the shapes of human-sized
insects. Once awake, the narrator understands that he has been chosen
to join their ranks when one of his hands starts to turn into a pincer
and tentacles appear on his body. Another evil and ancestral cult is
discovered by the narrator of "The Last Feast of Harlequin" in
underground tunnels outside a small provincial town. He follows a
group of strange zombie-like clowns and sees with horror one of them
turn into a worm, soon followed by his peers.

Contamination is also able to transform a human into an object
– hardly a surprising phenomenon in a work that features so many
live puppets. In "Dr. Voke and Mr. Veech," Veech asks the doctor to
help him get revenge on the woman he loves and who has spurned
him for another. Dr. Voke obliges and seizes the two lovers as if they
were mere puppets. When they are brought down again, as if lowered
by the strings of a puppeteer, they are as one: "there is too much of
everything on this body. Two faces sharing a single head, two mouths
that have fallen silent forever with parted lips."[24] Another variation on
the same theme can be found in "In a Foreign Town, in a Foreign
Land," where the hotel of the mysterious Mrs. Pyk, already mentioned
earlier, contains treasures of circus costumes and accessories. When
the hotel's guest falls asleep in the clown costume he has

---

[23] Thomas Ligotti, *Songs of a Dead Dreamer and Grimscribe* (New York:
Penguin Books, 2015), 71.
[24] Ibid., 178.

surreptitiously put on, a strange vision greets him when he opens his eyes in the morning: he has been turned into a clown's head at the end of a stick that Mrs. Pyk is holding in her artificial hand.

One final principle of contamination can be found in Ligotti's stories, that of the dead invading the living, the inorganic seeping into the organic. This contamination takes on a slightly more evolved shape than that of the mere undead, the zombie, or even the vampire. With Ligotti, as with Lovecraft, this mutation has a deeply terrifying and disturbing effect, as I will explain in my next part. I will here only quote two examples among many. The characters of "The Shadow at the Bottom of the World" discover a scarecrow that looks alive. This scary vision is actually nothing compared to what is really happening: the scarecrow has been invaded by a black substance emerging from the depths of the earth:

> It was something *black* and twisted into the form of a *man*, something that seemed to have come up from the *earth* and *grown* over the wooden planks like a *dark fungus, consuming* the structure. There were now *black legs* that hung as if *charred* and *withered*; there was a *head* that *sagged* like a sack of *ashes* upon a *meagre body* of *blackness*; and there were thin arms stretched like *knobby branches* from a *lightning-scorched tree*. All of this was supported by a thick *dark stalk* which rose from the *earth* and reached into the effigy like a *hand* into a puppet.[25]

The lexical fields of humanity, of vegetation, and of death are here merged together in the description of this evil excrescence. The characters have found an entity that is not supposed to be because it reconciles categories that are normally separate and incompatible with the object they are occupying. In "The Red Tower," the last series of

---

[25] Ibid., 440, my emphasis.

objects produced by the eerie factory uses the same principle – it creates organisms born from graves scattered over the third basement of the building. Those "hyper-organisms" coalesce two fundamentally opposed characteristics: vitality and decomposition, life and death, "each of these hyper-organisms, even as they scintillated with an obscene degree of vital impulses, also, and at the same time, had degeneracy and death written deeply upon them."[26] Bodies in Ligotti's work are suffering bodies, mutating bodies, bodies which deny the codes of our reality.

II. Aesthetics of the fantastic for a metaphysical reading

Besides the fear of foreigners and of the decline of his race, already mentioned above, there was in Lovecraft an acute awareness of the absurdity of the world and of human purposelessness. Lévy develops this idea many times in his work dedicated to Lovecraft, as shown by the following: "The fantastic, after all, is perhaps nothing more than a heartrending revelation of the absurd, seeking to dislodge the reader from his normal states of mind and his familiar certitudes."[27] This comment perfectly fits Ligotti's work without the addition of the therapeutic purpose of writing that Lévy also detects in Lovecraft. In his non-fiction volume *The Conspiracy Against the Human Race*, Ligotti defends a pessimistic and nihilistic vision of the world, which provides insights for the reading of his fictional work. The author explains that the tragedy of man is the rise of his consciousness: what distinguishes him from other species is also his curse. Consciousness does nothing but reveal to man his condition and his inevitable death.

---

[26] Thomas Ligotti, *Teatro Grottesco* (London: Virgin Books Ltd, 2008), 74.
[27] Maurice Lévy, *Lovecraft, a Study in the Fantastic*, trans. S. T. Joshi (Detroit: Wayne State University Press, 1988), 32.

Any quest for meaning is therefore doomed to failure: our lives have no meaning, our actions have no meaning, our desire to stretch the limits of man are only absurd and laughable gesticulations, like those of a puppet. The function of dolls and marionettes in his stories is therefore easier to understand. Lévy had incidentally already defined the Gothic as a representation of human tragedy – at the end of his paper entitled "Aspects du corps gothique," he wrote:

> But [the Gothic] can also be, for those who believe a little in Darwin's message, this confiscation of individual freedom to the benefit of the evolution of the species as it is described by the stories written and told in the late nineteenth century. If one is only unwittingly and inescapably reenacting a particular human type while believing they are living an original existence, independent and free in their body, [...] then all life is likely to become the worst Gothic story.[28]

Ligotti's stories are therefore among those Gothic stories where the body becomes the symbol of the masquerade in which man wishes to play a role at any cost. For Ligotti, most of us live in a state of willing hypnosis, like the inhabitants of the town in "The Sect of the Idiot" who live under the influence of the insect-men who themselves worship an idiot god. Is it not the function of fools and clowns to distract and blind us so that we do not see reality, as the narrator from "The Last Feast of Harlequin" aptly notes?[29]

What to do when we become puppets as well, like poor Veech who, after witnessing what Dr. Voke did to the woman he loved, has no control over himself and can only laugh in unison with the

---

[28] Maurice Lévy, "Approches du Texte Fantastique," *Caliban* 16 (1979), 81.

[29] Thomas Ligotti, *Songs of a Dead Dreamer and Grimscribe* (New York: Penguin Books, 2015), 271.

Doctor's automaton? What to do when we come to understand that, contrary to what Dr. Voke claimed, the automaton is not a mere machine but instead represents our actual condition: we are the automatons? Certain characters receive a form of dark enlightenment like the narrator of "The Clown Puppet" who ultimately understands, after the puppet's numerous and absurd visits, that he is far from being the only person to be reserved such treatment. Quite the opposite: the absurdity of his situation is universal, as illustrated by his words: "I discovered how wrong I had been. Who knows how many others there were who might say that their existence consisted of nothing but the most outrageous nonsense, a nonsense that had nothing behind it or beyond it except more and more nonsense – a new order of nonsense, perhaps an utterly unknown nonsense, but all of it nonsense and nothing but nonsense."[30] When Ascrobius, in "In a Foreign Town, in a Foreign Land," understands the tragedy of human consciousness, he does not simply try to end his life, he attempts to find a way to entirely erase his existence, as if he had never been born. It is precisely this endeavour that makes him a monster rather than his physical deformity, according to his physician Dr. Klatt. Other characters find shelter in a dream of disembodiment allowing them to lose themselves in a vision of non-life and objectification. Such is the case of the traveller who sees himself as a clown's head at the end of Mrs. Pyk's stick. When he wakes up, after the initial terror caused by the dream, he asks Mrs. Pyk whether it will be possible for him to stay in the same room the next time he comes to town. When he does, the hotel has burnt down. Among the ruins are the charred corpses of travellers clad in costume clowns, all of them having seemingly preferred the dream of metamorphosis over the puppet show of reality in which we all play

---

[30] Thomas Ligotti, *Teatro Grottesco* (London: Virgin Books Ltd, 2008), 63.

a part. Will the narrator of "Dream of a Mannikin" succumb to the invitations of the shop window mannequins who, in his dreams, tirelessly repeat "Die into us"?[31] Are they inviting him to embrace a disembodiment that would allow him to escape reality, or are they encouraging him to accept his true nature, that of a plastic mannequin that reality is having fun clothing and stripping as it sees fit?

It might therefore be preferable still to actually leave the human world and thus renounce the "privilege" of consciousness. In "The Last Feast of Harlequin," the narrator visits a town during its strange carnival. A group of inhabitants sets itself apart from the rest of the population by wearing tattered clown costumes, faded and dirty. Ignored by the others, they symbolically become invisible before disappearing in the depths of underground tunnels which lead them to an impious altar where they can change into worms.

The other way out is death, if one has the courage to put an end to the masquerade, to the puppet show. After killing Veech, Dr. Voke starts dancing and shrieking erratically, his moves similar to those of a puppet, and finds a resolution to his crisis by falling to his death over the railing of his staircase. The only one left is the automaton, neither dead nor alive. His laughter has turned into howls and he is condemned to cry tears of blood and roll his insane eyes in the masquerade of existence. This masquerade oftentimes takes the form of a circus or puppetry show, but it can also take on different forms, such as those of the last series of objects produced by the factory in "The Red Tower." The hyper-organisms mentioned above – alive but decomposing – are a representation of our own condition. They are brought into the world by nameless "birthing graves," cast out into an

---

[31] Thomas Ligotti, *Songs of a Dead Dreamer and Grimscribe* (New York: Penguin Books, 2015), 57.

existence where they do not understand their purpose, condemned to live only to finally die.

Finally, the nightmarish principle which governs our lives is embodied in several ways in Ligotti's fiction. It is always a contaminating and insidious presence which feeds off everything and creeps in all places. In the film that is shown in the cinema in "The Glamour," this presence takes on the form of a woman who takes control of a man against his will like some sort of parasite: "His posture was rigid, betraying a state of paralysis, and his gaze was fixed, yet strikingly alive. 'She's showing us,' whispered the man who was sitting nearby me. 'That horrible witch has taken him. He cannot feel who he is any longer, only her presence within him'."[32] In "The Shadow at the Bottom of the World," the black organic substance that has invaded the scarecrow foreshadows the general decomposition and corruption which spreads over the city and transforms the autumn season into an endless canker of life and putrefaction, refusing to give way to winter. One final example can be found in "Nethescurial," in which the eponymous divinity is described as a presence that can be found in all things and all beings, likened to a voracious disease whose existence the narrator tries to deny:

> It is not a squirming, creeping, smearing shape I see upon the moon, not the shape of a great deformed crab scuttling out of the black oceans of infinity and invading the island of the moon, crawling with its innumerable bodies upon all the spinning islands of space. That shape is not the cancerous totality of all creatures, not the oozing ichor that flows within all things. *Nethescurial is not the secret name of the creation.*[33]

---

[32] Ibid., 411.
[33] Ibid., 333.

As a conclusion, I will briefly consider one final type of Gothic body in Ligotti's work: the text itself. While the Gothic text, or more generally the fantastic text, followed an evolution corresponding to a response to a social or cultural context (as seen before in Lévy's "Approches du texte fantastique" and "Aspects du corps gothique"), the brand of horror developed by authors like Lovecraft and Ligotti seems to materialise a nihilistic world vision. But while Lévy sees in Lovecraft the possibility to read the fantastic text as a means to reveal and then, maybe, to transcend the ambient irrationality and absurdity, Ligotti insists in *The Conspiracy Against the Human Race* on the absence of hope in his work. His stories are devoid of any trace of the potential comfort usually found in the recesses of horror literature, ever since the creation of the Gothic novel. Reading a story written by Ligotti is experiencing an immersion in a nightmarish reality. The reader should be careful lest the text, like an organic body, contaminate him. And what if any fantastic text, as Lévy writes at the end of "Approches du texte fantastique," was the writing of a gap, of a chasm? "With the authentic fantastic, which dares to explore its own limits, the text is the place where writing loses itself in the abyss that it has drawn to better tame that abyss – in other words, to better hide it."[34] In Ligotti's stories, the reader is always in danger of falling in that abyss, like the narrator in "Nethescurial." As a reader himself, since he reads the manuscript describing the cult of the divinity, he experiences the decline of his skepticism as the text that he holds in

---

[34] Maurice Lévy, "Approches du Texte Fantastique," *Caliban* 16 (1979), 15.

his hands contaminates him. The manuscript becomes a quasi-living body whose pages and architecture are compared to skin, bones and guts, and whose writing is likened to veins. When the narrator burns the text to get rid of it, the smoke that rises from it takes the shape of arms and heads. As he tries one final time to convince himself that his vision of the world is not corrupted by Nethescurial for ever, he cries out to no avail, "I am not dying in a nightmare."[35]

---

[35] Thomas Ligotti, *Songs of a Dead Dreamer and Grimscribe* (New York: Penguin Books, 2015), 333.

Bibliography

Cardin, Matt. "Liminal Terror and Collective Identity in Thomas Ligotti's 'The Shadow at the Bottom of the World'." In *The Thomas Ligotti Reader*, edited by Darrell Schweitzer, 85-100. Holicong: Wildside Press, 2003.

Dziemianowicz, Stefan. "'Nothing is What it Seems to Be': Thomas Ligotti's Assault on Certainty." In *The Thomas Ligotti Reader*, edited by Darrell Schweitzer, 38-52. Holicong: Wildside Press, 2003.

Goimard, Jacques. *Critique du fantastique et de l'insolite*. Paris: Pocket, 2003.

Lévy, Maurice. "Aspects du corps gothique : histoire, discours et fantasme." In *Les représentations du corps dans les œuvres fantastiques et de science-fiction : figures et fantasmes*, edited by Françoise Dupeyron-Lafay. 69-83. Paris: Michel Houdiard éditeur, 2006.

—. "Approches du Texte Fantastique." *Caliban* 16 (1979): 3-15.

—. *Lovecraft, a Study in the Fantastic*. Translated by S. T. Joshi. Detroit: Wayne State University Press, 1988.

Ligotti, Thomas. *Songs of a Dead Dreamer* and *Grimscribe*. New York: Penguin Books, 2015.

—. *Teatro Grottesco*. London: Virgin Books Ltd, 2008.

—. *The Conspiracy Against the Human Race*. New York: Penguin Books, 2018.

Price, Robert M. "The Mystagogue, the Gnostic Quest, the Secret Book." In *The Thomas Ligotti Reader*, edited by Darrell Schweitzer, 32-37. Holicong: Wildside Press, 2003.

Eyestalk

C. M. Crockford

O NE DAY WHILE at work my eyeball simply popped out of its socket. It was still attached to my optic nerve, so I was able to put it back into place, much like you would a loose part in an engine. But nevertheless, it was discomfiting.

I looked around to see whether anyone else could've seen this. No one was there as usual: All I could see were the rows of tan, symmetrical cubicle walls that dominated the floor, the fluorescent lights that sometimes shut on and off for no reason. I was also the only employee in this section aside from a woman named Rivers, though I had never seen her in person, and she made no apparent sounds as she worked. So I adjusted my left eye and turned back to my computer. I made two mental notes. One was that I could've sworn that I'd already turned down the overpowering glow of the screen in front of me, and two was to see a doctor about that eye problem. I rather liked this eye and didn't want to lose it.

"Well, to put it in layman's terms," the doctor told me a few days later, "Your left eye is, erm, dying." I shifted in my gown, unsure why she'd made me change into one in the first place. "Too much exposure to light and to digital screens. Quite common these days."

"Really?"

"Oh yes," she said cheerfully. I fidgeted in the chilly stir-ups my legs had been placed into. "Our jobs require an endless stimulation, total wear and tear on such delicate organs, such tender features. Fascinating isn't it?"

I said nothing. Her eyes were the color of a very fair blue marble I'd found once as a boy, and I couldn't help watching them move about. She ran her tongue over her teeth as she flipped through my charts and glided around the room.

"Um, is there anything I can do exactly to save my eye?"

"The best course of action would be to leave your job and avoid computers, I'm afraid. Likely no other way to keep it," she said as she took something out of her coat pocket, "but if you can't do that, this is a very nice way to appear presentable at work once it completely detaches." Her curls bobbed lightly as she handed me an eye patch. She beamed as I tried it on, the ribbon snapping against my scalp as the eye adjusted to darkness.

"Could I get out of these stir-ups, please?" She nodded, though she appeared to be disappointed, and hastened to remove them.

The next week at work, after my eye had spilled out of the socket three times, dangling off its wet rope until returned to order, I arrived at the fourteenth floor and knocked on the Boss' door. I heard his raspy voice call, "Come in, come in." I entered and saw his slender, sleek form in an oversized tux, his dark hair shining from some kind of lubricant. He was holding a small mirror to his face and powdering his nose.

"So, what can I help you with? Forgive me, I have a party to attend in about six hours."

"Frankly sir, I either need to transfer to a different department...or outright resign." I gulped. "It's my left eye, you see – it's falling out from the work I do here. Quite common apparently."

He glanced at me, raising an eyebrow. "I see. Well, I'm disappointed to hear this."

"Not that I'm unhappy here, sir, but-"

"Because the Company was *just* about to promote you."

"R-really?" My mind went blank. He put down his mirror and turned towards me.

"Why yes, a raise and everything, even an office. A damn shame if you left now, you know. You were just about to climb up another rung. You absolutely sure you'd want to leave us?"

"But – my eye..." I sputtered.

The Boss took a few paces forward, and now we were standing face to face. He gripped my shoulder, and I could feel it growing numb in his clutch. His voice was calm, intoxicating. "It's just an eye, nothing to write home about. You'll still have another to see with, friendo. And after all, isn't a bird's eye view on the third floor, some extra take home pay, so much bigger than one measly cornea?" I nodded gratefully. He released me and patted my arm. "Good man. Now if there's nothing else..." He returned to the mirror.

As I walked out of his office, the glare of the lights nearby was downright blinding, and then they slowly dimmed. As I adjusted to them, I could see only one other employee on this floor, working at her desk alone. There were spiraling, cold, dark circles under her eyes, and her hair seemed unkempt. She looked up from her computer and stared directly at me. Her eyes were oddly beautiful but as black as could be, the eyes of an ancient, porcelain toy. With her finger she pointed to her left eye and grinned. Her teeth were far too large for her mouth.

I broke away and quickly walked to the elevator, checking behind me every so often to see if she was still there. It wasn't until I turned the corridor that I was able to breathe again.

Eventually, I had the impaired eye removed in an operation, though I have kept it in a drawer under my desk. I occasionally look at that round piece of meat, white with thick lines of red, floating in the jar of formaldehyde, finding it oddly soothing. A small sacrifice for an office and a view of the large buildings that comprise the downtown area. I haven't seen the raise yet, but the new perks are well worth an eye patch and some mild adjustments to my sight.

Except now...now my right eye is starting to bother me.

The Mannequin Ideal

Andrew Koury

I T TAKES SEVERAL hours, hundreds of dollars' worth of software as well as the know-how to use it, aesthetic skill, and a culture's worth of conditioning to make a human attractive to other humans. It is only this final product that is worth consuming. How often this intangible image is in the minds of lovers to get them through the act of flesh. In most cases, it's considered a psychosexual supplement. A crutch. This is because the images these lovers consume are of the other sex. A way to commodify the horror of our bodies and beastly desires. But what of the those who desire the same sex? What happens when the unattainable is not a crutch, but your missing concept of self?

This is not a new issue. Before technical progress made the unreal more tantalizing real, we fetishized the abstract. The mannequin on display, dressed in current clothes. Some erroneously claim that the mannequins are blank so that you may place yourself within them. In fact, it is the opposite. The absence of the individual is the beauty. The absence of expression or emotion of any kind. The ultimate lack of self-awareness as the apex of attraction.

This is what I set out to become.

Before I thought this was possible, before I thought it desirable, I passed a storefront window. This was during a lull between both personal and national tragedies, so I had no plans or strong feelings about anything. My dreary life consisted of walking, working, and occasionally grasping at connection. All this to say that when I saw a tastefully colored collared shirt hugging the body of a mannequin on display in the storefront window, I was ready for it.

I was the only customer in the store. It was part of a chain of clothing stores. It was filled with collared shirts, t-shirts adorned with band names and logos popular a decade ago, and jeans and khakis. Or maybe there were more interesting things in the store. I wouldn't know. I walked straight to the mannequin.

At the end of the collar, pure unblemished, false skin shined at me. I picked up the same shirt from a stack of them on the table by the mannequin. I held it up in front of myself, trying to compare myself to the model. If I closed my eyes, I could pretend my skin didn't look so 'ethnic,' as my boss called it. My family calls it Lebanese. I call it irregular, as contrasted with the paragon before me. If I closed my eyes, I could pretend my stomach didn't protrude, that my skin was lighter, that I was taller, that I—

"Can I help you with anything, sir?" an old voice asked me, pulling me out of my fantasy/spiral.

"I was just admiring it," I answered. The old voice belonged to an older, pale man in nondescript dark clothing, which concealed what his body looked like. His name tag said 'Hi, my name is ____.'

"It is true beauty, isn't it?"

I looked at the old man. He had an intense sincerity in his voice, like he would lose something dear if I did not hear him.

"Oh yes. It truly is," I said.

"Everyone notices it. They stare, but they can't seem to look at it for long. I think they find it intimidating. But you don't turn away. You're not as narcissistic as them. So tell me, what do you see in it?" he stared at me as if waiting to hear a prophecy. But I was not an oracle, merely a confused young man.

"I like the blue color. It really stands out and catches the eye," I said.

He seemed to recede into himself. His intense stare was replaced by dead eyes and a blank smile.

"Oh, I see," he said. "Perhaps you would like to try it on?'

I went to the dressing room and tried on the shirt. I felt the profound disappointment of seeing what new clothes look like on a body like mine, bought the shirt, and walked through the dreary city to my apartment.

I'm told I think too much. I never know how to respond to this. Am I supposed to stop thinking? Go blank? Or simply abbreviate the thoughts I have into simple sentences? How do *they* know how much I'm thinking? Then I realize they aren't criticizing my thoughts, but my grim demeanor. If I put on a smile as the old man in the store did, the criticism goes away.

But I do know what they mean by the comment. I have a tendency to translate the world around me into terrifyingly blank atmospheres, to the point where I don't feel as if I am living in a world among people, but as a speck of dirt hidden in the carpet. It's not good to be this way for too long. Or maybe it is good in an ultimate sense, but it's certainly unsustainable in a normal life. So, I try to indulge in the other comment/imperative I often receive: "You need to get laid."

I met Damon a week ago on a hook up app. We texted back and forth and exchanged pictures and found each other to be enough for our purposes. I arrived at his door in my new shirt. I began to feel nervous. My breath was hurried, and it felt good to breathe. It was one of the few times I had felt something in a long time.

He came to the door and let me in. He got us both drinks.

"You look just as wound up as you do in your pictures, man," he told me.

And he looked just as wild as he did in his. He was a bear with long, black, shoulder length hair that he didn't seem to know or care had gone out of fashion in the eighties. Same with the chest hair sprouting from his undershirt.

A drink later we were in the bedroom.

I was never sure how to begin these encounters, but he was. He leaned in, eyes already closed and kissed me. I kissed back. Soon it was like we were each tugging at something invisible between our lips. Our clothes were off. He rubbed his hand against my shoulder. It occurred to me that I hadn't had physical contact with another person in months.

I started to pull away to say something. I'm good at talk in situations like this, nowhere else. But he pulled me back in close with a grunt. I remembered that we were still kissing. I didn't feel any pleasure with my tongue, just the wet smoothness of flesh. But his hand, which had descended from my shoulders to my back, felt like water drizzling through indentations on a sidewalk, beginning to gradually shape it in erosion.

I pulled him closer and rubbed my hands against his shoulders like he had with mine. It worked; he held me tighter. The two of us together, we were a living thing as one. Better than any individual. His body felt strong like a shield or like a shirt, tightening me into its shape. I was almost shaped into something of pure animal desire. Aware of the feelings but nothing else.

We smelled of sweat on skin, and I didn't mind at all.

He pushed me off the bed and onto the floor. He gripped the back of my head and pushed me towards his crotch.

I began to fulfill the obvious implication of the action. It was strange, there was nothing to prepare me for any action like this, pleasuring a body part left to the imagination in nearly all contemporary portrayals of men. I missed Damon's hands over me. I pulled away.

I was shoved back, hard. I realized just how little control I had. I would be shaped into anything he liked, whether I liked it or not. I looked up at him, hoping he would stop. My glasses were hanging low on my nose, so his face was blurred beyond recognition. All I saw was fuzzy white skin covering a sphere at the top of the torso on the top of the penis, which now seemed to pierce the back of my throat.

I adjusted again, hoping for mercy, but he shoved me in deeper. The sweat and the skin. The hands. The physical connection. It was all too much. Luckily, my mind was smarter than my animal self. I went blank, like Damon's face from my disadvantaged angle. I stopped feeling the heat, the contact, the sweat, the action. In the moment, all my newfound feeling disappeared.

I completed the action and was told I was a good fuck.

By the time I regained awareness of sensation, I was drenched. I didn't know how long I had been walking, didn't want to. I wanted to be lost in action. No, not that. I wanted to be blank. I didn't want to think about any kind of action.

I peeled my shirt away from my chest and felt grosser than before. It was hot and rainy. The raindrops cluttered up my glasses. I wiped the lenses clean and saw the mannequin in the storefront window before me.

In seeing the mannequin the first time, I felt the sadness of seeing an object of beauty one can never even hope to aspire to. A scolding perfection that fills one with a dejected longing and a soft promise to be better. When I bought the now drenched shirt, since ruined by its contact with a human, I felt like a deformed factory reject putting on a higher price tag in the hopes of fooling others and myself. Now, seeing the mannequin a second time, I realized that it couldn't see me. Why would it need to? It sensed nothing. Felt nothing. Never experienced sensation of any kind. As pain dampened my soul like so many raindrops, I felt an envy I no longer bothered to conceal behind shame.

I went inside to touch the mannequin, hoping that if it couldn't feel me, then I couldn't feel it.

Before I could do so, the old man put a hand on my shoulder, sending a sharp pain of adrenaline down my body.

"Can I help you?" he asked. I saw, now that were standing so close to one another, that his face was stretched. Not to the smooth ends of perfection, but it was clear that was the attempt. His hair was not natural; it was dyed. I could not tell if the attempts to look smoother helped his looks, or merely lengthened the distance between himself and the ideal, only that he was aware of the same things as me. "Can I help you?" he repeated with the same, practiced cadence of a sales worker.

"I wanted to see it. To touch it," I answered, surprised at the sound of my own voice. It was an absurd desire. I mentally prepared to leave in embarrassment.

"Why do you want to touch it?" he asked with that intensity from before.

I wanted to be it. "I need to."

He nodded. "If you're serious, I'll begin the preparations. Are you sure?"

"Yes," I said without a second's pause.

He began by bringing the closing gate down across the storefront's door and windows. He turned off the store lights and set up spotlights on the ground, looking up to the mannequin. He painted the blank human shaped canvas in golden light. First on the left side of the face, then a smaller light on the right. A kicker at the back. He used the store's shirts to block the light just so. It was perfect.

"Touch it," he said from black space, for I could see nothing but the mannequin.

93

In my anticipation, I began to experience feelings of danger and pleasure again. Suspended in black space, I looked the mannequin up and down once more and shivered, despite the heat of the lights. If I could feel this strongly again, should I truly give it up for the perfect experience of the unthinking? I coughed and felt the pain and dryness in my throat, remembering that feelings of excitement are simply the preamble to extraordinary pain.

I reached and touched the shoulder of the mannequin. To my disappointment, it felt cold, despite the lights shining on it. This reminded me of how hot I felt in the light. How damp and sweaty I was. How disgusting.

Then the pain eased from my body and mind. I began to feel the absence of dampness, but not dryness. Nothing came to replace the negative sensations in my blood. But as these things left me, the mannequin grew warm. I realized I could not hear anything. Smell anything. At last, I could no longer feel anything. The last experience I had was seeing my reflection in the gated storefront window. It gradually disappeared as the mannequin glowed brighter.

Death & The Maiden IV
Tatiana Garmendia

Daddy's Departure

Danielle Hark

Your apartment – waiting
for your death – it reeked of you.
Sweet Australian sunscreen, after-
shave and hair spray.

I reached for you, stepping
forward, three stories high,
towards the vast reservoir, when:
My hand encountered
the glass – your face
smooth and newly shaven.

I must let you go. You must
let you go. I do – you do –
The glass lets you go.

The Sprite House

Trent Kollodge

PAPER THIN SLIVERS of wood curled and fell to the cool floor, slowly sloughing away to reveal the complicated pattern of the sprite-house roundel. Mike's mind wandered in a meditative focus, a million miles away from the rhythmic movement of the blade in his hands. No thought intruded, no awareness of self or surroundings, just the lyrical susurration of the void, and the whorls of the wood.

"What are you making, Daddy?"

Mike jumped. The chisel slipped, gouged his thumb, and dragged his mind back from oblivion. Worse still, it sliced through the delicate carvings of the rosewood roundel. "Fuck." A shadow in the corner of his vision slipped off the end of the work bench and slithered into the cluttered corner, another flitted into the darkness above the rafters. "God damn it." He had been so close. Seven times he had attempted the roundel without a flicker of interest, and this time, not one, but two sprites had come to his woodworking song. *So fucking close.*

"Are you okay, Daddy?" Zoe asked.

The innocent concern of her voice drained the frustration from Mike's system like the proper dosage of a good pharmaceutical. He looked down at his thumb and squeezed. Bright blood dripped onto the concrete floor. It wasn't her fault. When she needed him, she needed him. A good father would be there for her. "What are you doing up, sweetie? It's way past your bedtime."

"You were making a noise," she said, her worried eyes never leaving the blood. "It woke me up."

"What kind of noise?" Mike asked, pulling a handkerchief from his back pocket and wrapping it around his thumb until the stain stopped soaking through. The ache throbbed, but he didn't think it needed stitches.

"Like a song: 'rahmmmmmm,' but really loud."

"I don't remember that," he said. "But I guess I kind of space-out sometimes when I'm working. Let's get you back to bed."

Zoe took his good hand and let herself be led back through the kitchen and down the hall to her bedroom, stopping only to potty, wash her hands, sip the top of a tall glass of water, and rescue Christopher Bear from the tangled clutches of the blanket on the couch. She waited until Mike's finger touched the light switch before asking, "Daddy, were you working on the sprite house again?"

"Last piece," he said, forcing a smile, "and then it's done."

"And will the sprites come?"

"That's what it's for."

"And they'll take us away to fairyland?"

"Just you, my pet, sprites don't come for grownups, too heavy." He patted his belly with a feigned pout, and stepped a foot into the hall.

"I don't want to go alone," Zoe called behind him.

"You won't even miss me," he said, clicking out the light.

"Daddy," she called from the darkness, "will Mommy be in fairyland?"

"It's ten thirty, sweetie. Go to sleep."

"But do you think Mommy will be there?"

"Goodnight."

On the way back to the garage, Mike stopped to tape his thumb up properly. The haggard man in the mirror caught his eyes. "It's important not to lie," he whispered, "even if Kara would disagree." Zoe's mother would have lied to the moon and back to comfort a child, any child, even a grown up one. Maybe all good parents lied. Maybe all good people did. He couldn't bring himself to lie though, not to Zoe, not about important things. *God damn, I'm going to miss that girl,* he thought, swallowing hard. But if the promise of the Manual were true, he wouldn't miss her at all; that was the whole point. He turned away from the mirror's gaze.

The roundel was ruined, of course. The slip had cut too deep into the image to work around, and sprites didn't allow repairs: no glue, no nails, no splinting to fill the gap. The intricate knot of leaves and thorns had to be carved of a single piece of unblemished wood, and cut in a single session, without deviation from the pattern.

I can't do this, Mike thought. He tossed the failed creation on the scrap pile beneath the bench and cracked open a beer.

Tilting his head back in a long pull, he studied the rafters where the second sprite had disappeared. There was no evidence of its passage. Mike never saw them arrive either; they just eased into his peripheral vision, pretending to be a tool on the wall, or an empty bottle at the end of a shelf, until the spell of the work was broken or completed, and then they skittered back into the shadows from whence they had come.

Or the mind whence they had come, Mike thought, wondering again if the sprites were only a hallucinatory side effect of the Sprite House Manual. The work certainly had a trance-inducing effect. He flipped through the brittle, yellowed pages once again, studying the hand-penciled diagrams and instructions. The methods it described were exacting, precise, hypnotic, but had done more to calm the raging chemicals of Mike's depressive spells than any medication his doctors had prescribed. Selfishly, he wondered what he would do with himself when the project was complete.

Closing the Manual, Mike swigged his beer again, and eyed the work in progress. The sprite house was a hideous thing; disturbingly intricate, and twisted to an alien aesthetic that defied comfort, as if sketched from the hind-brain's hidden language of disquieting emotions. Birch saplings had been stripped of bark, soaked, twisted, and forced into an off-kilter framework with specific knots of willow bark strapping. Hand-carved beads of bone, dyed with everything from berries to crushed insects, had been strung and hung in peculiar patterns that suggested faces, or feces, or feminine figures, depending on the light and the angle. Ricks of horsetail, each strand carefully washed and counted, had been woven, braided, and draped like thatching for the roof. And a patternless jigsaw of river stone tiling had been meticulously sorted for size and color, and grouted into the floor inside, a hidden symbol etched beneath each stone. One cubit tall and twice as wide, the house lurked on a sawhorse table at the far side of the garage, needing only the roundel above its door to make it complete. Would it work? Would it call sprites to take the child? Or would its promise flit away like an illusion, like the sprites themselves? Mike didn't know which to hope for more. *I'll screw it up somehow,* he thought. *I always do.*

Tossing a loose tarp over the house, Mike punched the broken plastic button that opened the garage door. The summer night rushed in behind the chain driven clatter with a warm press of cricket song. Across the street, the dim light of a neighboring garage spilled out onto a driveway, the thick silhouette of a heavy man clearly visible next to the stout square of a cooler: Alan was up and looking for company.

Mike pretended to inspect the gutters, but Alan's arm was already waving. Mike kept his shoulders from visibly drooping as he breathed a heavy sigh. *A good neighbor would be happy to chat,* he thought. *And you know damn well Alan won't take 'no' for an answer.* Halfheartedly returning the wave, he grabbed the remains of his twelve pack, clicked off the light, and headed over.

"Evenin' Mike. Been a while since you've been by," Alan said, looking older than his twenty-seven years. "Throw those bad boys in the cooler and grab yourself a chair."

"Thanks," Mike said, grateful as always that Alan would take the brunt of the conversation upon himself.

Mike sat, drank, and watched the lack of traffic on the sleepy street, while Alan maintained the small talk, and they made a game of crushing their empties and tossing them toward the bin by the curb. A reluctant moon peaked over the suburban skyline to give the streetlights some competition as the alcohol loosened their tongues and settled their limbs into a melancholy turn.

"You see that thing in the news about the woman in Alabama?" Alan asked. "What she did to those kids?"

"I saw it," Mike said, disgusted.

"Almost makes me glad I don't have kids. Too much worry."

"No one should have kids in a world like this."

"Says the hypocrite," Alan snorted.

"You didn't know Zoe's mother," Mike said. "She was very... convincing."

"Of course, I knew Kara," Alan said, leaning forward to study his beer for a while. "No offense, Mike, but Kara was a train wreck. What did you see in that woman?"

Mike smirked at Alan's gentle euphemism. Most people just called her a slut, or worse, and never bothered to ask past the size of her breasts or the extent of her crazy. "Deep down, she was a good person," he said.

Alan huffed. "Don't kid yourself, Mike. Kara was a liar and a flake. And she skipped out on you with the first loser she felt sorrier for than your dumb ass."

"Kara died."

"Of course, she did, after she left you, after months of..."

Mike stared at the concrete and let the accusations wash by. It wasn't Kara's fault she left him; after all, who could stay with someone like him?

So few people had been able to see the truth of Kara, and there was never a point in trying to convince them of it. Mike knew though; Kara had been a beacon in the darkness. Who else could gaze unblinking into the shit-pool of humanity and still find hope? Who else could envision a bright future from the muddle of the world without the pretense or illusions that held most people afloat? Who else could touch the bleak damage of Mike's soul and still find something worth loving? "She had a way of seeing things," he said, looking up at the stars, "that almost made being here worthwhile."

"Oh, don't give me that depression shit," Alan said. "I know you don't mean it. I've seen you doting on that little girl of yours. She lights up the whole world for you, and you know it."

Mike felt the truth of the words grapple a knot of guilt in his chest and throat. Much of his fatherly doting was a sham, a pale mimicry of what would have come naturally to Kara, an act to meet the expectations of what he *should* be, but could never be. And yet, he did love the girl. Even the thought of someone harming his Zoe was enough to make him sick to his stomach. And the thought of her gone... He turned away and drowned the selfish thought in a half-can swallow. "Doing right by Zoe and wishing her the suffering of existence are two different things," he said.

Alan tensed up and studied Mike's face intently for half a beat. "You're still building that sprite house, aren't you?"

"What?" Mike said. A shock of fear hit his gut as if he'd been caught sewing doves' eyelids shut for the cruelty of it. No one knew about the house but Zoe.

Alan twisted the beer can in his hands around and around. He raised it to his mouth, frowned to keep his lips from quivering, and swallowed hard. "I should never have given you that manual," he said. "It ought to be destroyed."

Mike forced a laugh—the sudden threat to his hopes bringing their possible reality into a sharp focus. "It's a fool's pastime at best.

A joke. No one believes in fairies."

"You're a terrible liar, Mike. Those shadowy fuckers are already messing with your memories. Hell, you can't even keep Kara straight in your head." Alan finished his beer, crushed the can, and walked a wavering line to the curb, taking time to pick up all of the near misses along the way.

Mike watched and fidgeted with his own can. How did Alan know about the Sprite House Manual? Zoe could have told him, but that didn't seem likely; the two never said more than a brief hello. And what was this about Alan giving him the Manual? Alan hadn't given him the Manual, he had got it from... where had he got it? Mike couldn't remember. It had always been a part of him, hadn't it?

"The thing is, Mike," Alan said, suddenly sitting again in the chair next to Mike. "The thing is, I don't think I just found that manual, I think I used it."

Implications hung in the night air between them. Alan had no children. Mike had known Alan for years, and knew damn well that Alan had never had children.

"I don't remember specifics," Alan said, "fat or thin, brunette or blond, happy or serious the way they sometimes are. I think she was a girl, but even that's conjecture. Hell, I don't even know which of my exes could have been the mother or if we lived in this house or at my old apartment. I can't remember a single thing, not one blessed detail. And no one else does either. Just like the Manual says; it's like she never existed. But there's a hole, Mike, a hole in my heart that nothing fills, a hole that was once a child. Don't ask me how I know." He turned to Mike, guilty tears hanging in agonized eyes. "You can't do this thing, Mike. You have to stop."

"You don't understand," Mike said. "I'm not doing it for me."

Anger twitched into Alan's posture, shoulders tensing, hand straining against the hard plastic of the chair. Mike could see all the sentimental arguments for progeny welling up behind his pursed lips; all the DNA lies that whispered absurdities of hope just to push the species into the future, no matter the cost. None of it stood up against the crushing horrors of the human condition. The crushing horrors that Zoe would soon have to face. The very horrors from which the sprite house offered release, not death, not abduction, but a fairyland of pure non-existence; wiping a child clean out of the past, present, and future; never conceived, never born, never existing at all. Mike didn't want to argue; people rarely understood. "Gotta piss," he said, getting up and navigating the mess of Alan's garage to the inside door.

Alan's house was a mirror image of his own, though the cheap bachelor furniture left it feeling vacant in a way Mike's home never did. "Spartan," Kara would have called it with a generous lie. Mike stumbled his way to the bathroom and laughed at the foreignness of the toilet seat being up. *Selfish bastard would probably leave it up even if he had a daughter,* Mike thought as he aimed his stream against the sway of his inebriation. People like that didn't deserve children in Mike's opinion; they had no empathy.

Returning through the garage, Mike found Alan's chair empty, and the man himself nowhere to be seen. *Maybe he just stumbled off to bed,* Mike hoped. It was a pleasant thought. Mike folded the chairs, leaned them against the wall, and dragged the cooler back inside. Then he clicked off the light and pulled the garage door shut, happy to be rid of the confrontation he had been bracing for. Happier still to have the hope of the sprite house feel that much more real. Halfway down the drive, a flicker of light caught the corner of his eye.

In the narrow passage between Alan's garage and the neighboring fence, the tall, bright flames of lighter-fluid-soaked paper roared up from an open barbecue grill. The low-angle light painted Alan's face demonic. "It had to be done, Mike," he said. "I can't let you make the same mistake I did."

Mike looked down in time to see the last of the curling patterns of the Sprite House Manual before the pages blackened completely and consigned their secrets to the smoke. The aborted roundel was there too, charring amidst the consuming flames. Despair cut through the alcohol in Mike's blood, through the anger, and through the last of his hopes. He took three full breaths before turning and walking home; a sixty-three-step journey that might have taken eternity. His body felt numb. The world around him hushed. The sprite house had been a feeble hope, like an atheist's prayer or a flower on a loved one's grave, but it had been *his* hope, the last lifesaver in the wake of Kara's death.

The next few days were a haze, muffled and muted by the loss; a return to the depression that had haunted him before the Manual had come into his life, a sliding into the desolation he had lived in before Kara had found him. Caffeine and force of habit got him through the routine, but each repetition grew harder, each passing conversation less genuine, each smile weaker. He could barely look in his daughter's eyes without seeing the suffering that awaited her; abandoned by her mother, genetic predisposition to depression and neglect from her father, a physical beauty to attract the worst of a sexist society. Every day she grew more aware, more capable of suffering not just the frailties of physical pain in a world of distracted drivers, decreasing water, rape culture violence, and antibiotic-resistant disease, but the mental anguishes of heartache, loneliness, outrage, and guilt. *How long until the cruel meaninglessness of life slaps her in the face and twists that innocence to the ugly truth of the utter indifference of the world?*

"What's wrong Daddy?" Zoe said, sitting and patting his shoulder with the paw of her stuffed bear.

He wanted to turn away, to curl up and cry. He could never be the father she needed, never be worthy of her love. And now, he couldn't even give her the one thing he had hoped to achieve; the peace that she deserved. "I didn't want to tell you, sweetie, but I can't finish the sprite house."

"Why not?" she said, squeezing his hand.

"A bad man burned the manual, and I can't remember what the last piece looks like."

"You mean the round thorny knot?"

"That's the one; it was very complicated."

Zoe's brow furrowed the way it had when she'd discovered that her favorite food had once been a living, grazing cow; the moment she had chosen vegetarianism without taking another bite. She swallowed hard and said, "It looked just like the song you sang."

"I don't remember the song either," Mike said.

"I do. Get your wood and chisel, and I'll sing it for you."

"That's silly. I can't carve a song."

Zoe jumped up, full of enthusiasm, and started to pull him toward the garage. "Come on, Daddy. Of course you can."

Mike pulled himself together to humor the child. It was the least he could do. *A good father would smile and make it all better,* he thought. *She deserves so much more.*

While she led him through the house she prattled on, regurgitating all the encouraging phrases she had picked up from him in her short years. "You can do it Daddy. You're super good at carving. Even Christopher Bear thinks so. And don't worry, I'm sure sprites are like fairies, and *they* don't see with their *eyes*; they feel with their *hearts*. I'm sure you'll get it just right."

Once Mike was settled into his workbench with a newly sharpened chisel and a virgin block of rosewood in hand, Zoe stood back and began to sing. Her voice had always been husky for a child, and its dark, wavering timbre suited the slowly droning hum well. At first, the song seemed to go nowhere, and it was all Mike could do to keep from putting the wood down and suggesting the distracting bribe of a movie and ice cream. But the determined look in Zoe's eye told him that she wouldn't let him go that easily, so he took a deep breath, and began to carve.

What did it look like? he thought as he made the first tentative cuts. He couldn't remember, couldn't picture the page in the Manual with any accuracy at all. There had been thorns, yes, and knotted vines, but how many thorns? Had they curved clockwise or counter? Had the knot turned on itself six or eight times as it twisted around the circle? Seven times he had attempted the carving; how had the pattern not worked its way into his memory?

It doesn't matter, the dream is gone. What mattered was that he carve something, anything, for his Zoe. She was putting in such an effort, not because she wanted the sprite house, but because she knew he wanted to make it for her. Just like her mother. And as his thoughts wandered to Kara, to his Zoe, the chisel in his hand caught the song again, gently curving along half envisioned lines. They weren't the same lines he had carved before, he knew, but they were the right lines; as if the meaning, and not the form, were what mattered.

Shadows moved in the corners of his vision, but Mike didn't look, didn't break the spell of the song. Instead, he lifted his own voice to join that of his daughter's, harmonizing low to her slow melodic wandering, letting the steel of the blade shear away at the fragrant wood as the lapping waves of the oblivion song washed away the world around them.

Then the blade lifted, and the shadows skittered away. The roundel sat perfect in his palm.

"Is it done?" Zoe asked, her voice cracking hoarse.

"Yes." He said. "It came out just right."

She leaned over and studied the delicate carving, its spiraling thorns and woven stems. "How do you know?" she asked.

"The sprites came to watch. Did you see them?" Mike pointed to the rafters with his eyes.

Zoe looked him straight in the eye and nodded. "Do you want to put it on the house?"

"If you do."

Again, Zoe nodded, her face determined. Together they took the roundel to the house and placed it in the waiting frame. Now complete, the house seemed to throb with a life of its own. The intricacies of the roundel knot pulsed with illusory movement, as if each carved vine constricted and moved in peristaltic waves that radiated out through the twisted frame of the construction, shifting the hanging beads and sending ripples through the horsetail roof. Outside, the crickets hushed.

"Will the sprites come now?" Zoe asked, a slight tremor in her voice.

111

"They'll come," Mike said, looking into her blue eyes. "But they won't know who to take with them unless you mark the door with a drop of blood."

Zoe's lip set tight and she hugged her bear. "Will it hurt?"

"Yes, but only a little."

"Okay, but do it quick."

Mike held the chisel by the blade so that just the tiniest point protruded from between his fingers. The jab was deft and quick, and before she even felt it, Zoe wiped her finger across the tiny door.

The summer chorus of cricket song rose shrill and insistent in the darkness. Mike opened his eyes and wiped the tears from his face. He didn't know why he was crying, but sometimes depression was like that; pure chemical imbalance without reason. He let out a deep, shuddering sigh and eyed the inane clutter of his lonely garage: stacks of boxes, a dirty workbench, and this monstrosity on the makeshift table. "So ugly," he said to the empty room. "What was I thinking?" He couldn't remember why he'd started such a thing.

Trying to shake the gaping emptiness from his heart, Mike dragged the plastic trash bin over, and began breaking the sprite house apart. His toe kicked something soft on the floor. "Where did you come from?" Mike asked the stuffed bear. The hole in his heart ached deeper, but he ignored the unwanted debilitation as pointless and unrelated. He tossed the bear in among the broken sticks and tangled beads. *Probably belongs to one of the neighbor kids,* he thought, *maybe I can fish it out later and leave it by the curb.*

Dragging the bin down to the street, Mike was unable to avoid Alan, who was bustling over to meet him.

"Sorry about the other night," Alan said. "Too many beers. I don't know what I was thinking."

"No problem. The house was a stupid idea anyway."

"Come by tonight, and I'll make it up to you?"

"Sure," Mike said. There was no point in arguing. No point at all.

Sirens in the Night

Paul L. Bates

S IRENS IN THE night. Always distant; always at 3:30 AM.

I remember Dr. Watt telling me to think of the Sirens in Greek mythology. The sisters, he intoned—each half bird, half woman—lured men to their island. He said I should allow my sirens to lure me deeper into comforting sleep. He smiled broadly, nodded slowly and sagaciously, certain his allusion would be of great use to me. I blinked, not certain I comprehended. I'm unsure, but I vaguely remember that those alluring mythological creatures enticed unsuspecting mariners to their doom, their minds addled by the Siren song, their ships dashed to pieces upon the rocks. I must look it up.

The sirens fade eventually. I become aware of that other sound they masked. The McGurk's screaming baby in the next apartment across the common corridor. Between the sirens and the screaming my headache has returned with a vengeance. And my insomnia as well. I need something stronger than those little yellow caplets Dr. Watt has prescribed.

The new capsules he gave me are much larger. Pink with blood red bands binding the two halves together. His own unnamed concoction, he averred. I cannot pry them apart.

I still awaken every morning at 3:30, however.

For an hour I toss and squirm. My eyes pop open, like faulty window shades. When I peer at the ceiling, it is churning, undulating, reminding me of spiraling water in a toilet. Then a sudden nausea washes over me. Unable to move, I close my eyes, feel my pores exude an icy, foul smelling sweat. After a few minutes, I take a chance, stare at the ceiling again, watch it change color from its typical evening ashen cream to a neon red as it captures the glint of passing taillights penetrating the blinds. But it no longer wobbles. The dizziness has passed. I heave a heavy sigh.

But now the McGurk's baby is crying again. A few minutes later the headache begins anew. I wrap my head in the pillow, trying to blot out the noise.

Dr. Watt insists I do not call him for two weeks. *Give the new medication a chance to take hold,* he says. Take hold of what?

It's been two weeks tomorrow. I still awaken at 3:30, dizzy, nauseous, immobile, bathed in a reeking, cold sweat, the lamentation of distant sirens fading. And when they pass, the next headache starts on cue. As I acclimate to the stabbing pain, I notice it feels like there is something very much alive trying to break free from within my cranium—something small and determined pushing and thrashing upward at the top of my head with a savage insistence that will not be denied; clawing and picking its way free no matter what the cost to me. I rub my crown absently, feel a small swelling, a tiny, painful pimple, growing larger while I rub.

I gasp, sit up, certain the top of my head is about to explode; certain I am being excavated. The baby begins shrieking in earnest. I've never heard it this loud before. There is an abrupt pounding at my temples. I cannot breathe—I'm suffocating. I'm certain I'm about to die. I want to scream but cannot remember how. Everything is coming undone...

In the morning, free of the pain, that's all I can recall about the previous night.

The pimple is gone.

That evening, when I return home from work, Mrs. McGurk is waiting for me in the common corridor. Choking on her sorrow, she tells me the baby died last night. Her eyes are pink and swollen with grief. Her voice is cracked and broken. For a long moment, we stare at one another in bleak silence.

Horrible, I blather my condolences; awkwardly embrace her. Even shed some tears.

Still, maybe now I can sleep.

Pausing on the front stoop the next evening, I discern just how the inner city has grown so much taller without my noticing, as if it was done in secret. For the first time, I am aware of the many construction cranes hovering above climbing, steel skeletons to the north and the south. Distant, creeping shadows have become so much darker as the man-made canyons grow deeper. We are multiplying at a prodigious rate. What are we doing? Where will it end? Somewhere an ambulance lends its familiar lament to my casual observation.

I have slept through the night for the past week.

I am feeling unusually at peace, as if I have actually grown lighter, less dense. I must find a scale to weigh myself.

No need to speak with Dr. Watt. His pills seem to be working.

It's happening again. Have I developed a resistance to the new medication already?

The Braggs are screaming at one another in the apartment immediately above me. There is a rage in his voice matched by a vehemence in hers. Soon my headache is back. Once again, it feels like something is trying to break free from within the confines of my skull. Once more, there is a small, painful lump on my crown, swelling as I run a finger across it. Once again, a determined throbbing at my temples. Once again, I am short of breath, certain I am about to die.

How long does it last? Forever?

Then the sirens, this time in the street below.

Then nothing—blessed oblivion.

Distant thunder. Or maybe just heavy boots on the stairs. Am I asleep or awake? Is there really a difference? And then again nothing until the alarm sounds.

There is still a commotion within and without when I go to work; police techs scrambling up and down the stairs; gawking spectators, patrol cars and vans blocking the street as I hurry to the subway. My own apathy to whatever has happened surprises me.

It's terrible, Mrs. McGurk sobs that evening, accosting me on the stoop. The Braggs have gored one another with kitchen knives. Multiple times. Even the police were baffled. How could they have continued mutilating each other with such odious determination in that horrific state? How will she ever remove the blood stains from the carpet, the walls, the woodwork—even the ceiling? How will she be able to rent that ruined apartment to someone new? How much tragedy can possibly occur in such a confined area? Where will it end? So many philosophical questions. So many ways to cope with her grief.

Once again, I commiserate with her, utterly indifferent, strangely at peace, oddly lighter than ever before. She cocks her head to one side, as if to study my face, unsure what is different about me. Our conversation ends abruptly.

The upstairs apartment remains empty.

Mrs. McGurk has grown pale and sullen.

Mr. Schlock, the tenant who lives in the basement apartment directly below us has taken to playing his stereo loud at all hours. His taste in music is quite eclectic. Horns, guitars, electronics, symphony orchestras, brass bands, jazz combos, vocalists, angry poets—there seems no end to the variety. Perhaps he seeks a voice to follow.

Yet all of it feels so distant, impersonal, save the endless, loud music when I am trying to sleep.

Then another night's dreaming abruptly terminated at 3:30. Another bout of dizziness, nausea, cold sweat, headaches, pimple, gasping, collapse, sirens in the night.

Mr. Schlock has slit his wrists to the gloomy tones of Mozart's Requiem, Mrs. McGurk confides somberly that evening as I climb the outside steps. She has been waiting nervously in the foyer for my return. I simply nod, as if I had expected it.

Her eyes delve into mine for answers I cannot give her.

Dr. Watt has left a message. His voice is more jovial than I remember it. He asks to see me again, at my convenience, *the sooner the better*. For an *update*, he calls it. I hear him giggling as the machine switches off.

I see him during my lunch break the next day. He is more cheerful than I have ever know him, positively ecstatic. "Tell me everything," he insists, all smiles, ushering me to a chair. "Leave nothing out." He rubs his large hands together in an archaic gesture.

I tell him in great detail about the headaches, the cold sweats, the dizziness, the pimples, the shortness of breath, the loss of memory, certain that is what he expects of me.

"Is that all?" he demands, waving a large hand to stop me in midsentence. His voice is stern and reprimanding. His eyes are accusing and angry. His hands clench into mammoth fists. Dr. Watt is a most intimidating figure when displeased.

After a moment's reflection, I tell him about the seemingly coincidental catastrophes that inevitably follow each episode.

"Ah," he purrs. "That's more like it."

I take that to mean he is glad that I have withheld nothing from him.

It has been a week since the McGurks were found mummified in their apartment.

The police had so many questions I could not answer to their satisfaction. Had I spoken with the McGurks recently? Why not? Did I ever visit them? Why not? Did I smell anything odd last Friday—gas maybe? Did I smell anything more recently, like rotting meat? Did I think it odd all the other tenants have died one after the other?

To that I replied everyone dies sooner or later, as far as I know. The lead detective told me I was a very strange man. I smiled, a smile of understanding.

I'm certain he misunderstood.

I feel ever so much lighter—if that is even possible—as if I could just float away.

No one has rented the three vacant apartments.

No one cleans the stairs and common corridor anymore. They are accumulating fluffy, purple dust balls and swaths of gritty dirt.

I have lost track of time. Has it been weeks, months or longer since I last spoke with Dr. Watt?

However, the pattern remains the same. That part of it has a continuity I can identify. The rest of it has none. I sleep soundly for a week or two before each bout of insomnia. I don't remember exactly how many times the pattern has repeated itself. What I do know is that it happens a lot. As I said before, it's always the same. There is no variation, not even a little. My sleep is abruptly punctuated by an acute nausea as I watch the ceiling spinning. Then the cold sweat, headache, pimple, asphyxia and collapse. Sirens wailing in the night, on and on, swelling ever closer. Oblivion.

Silent men in white hazmat suits carrying all manner of peculiar instruments came to my apartment building on several occasions, aiming their meters, wands and tubes at everything, looking to measure who knows what, perhaps their own consistency. They leave without asking anything; without revealing anything.

I remember I read in the paper there was some manner of epidemic. *A plethora of death* the author called it—murder, suicide, and the *grotesquely* inexplicable. So many ways to describe bewilderment. He went on to say someone of note was preparing a television documentary. Someone else of greater note was writing a book, hoping for a film. The journalist wondered how this ghastly tale could be properly told with no end to the calamity in sight. Apparently, the phenomena are not limited to this neighborhood, either. *Over three dozen epicenters of unimaginable catastrophe,* the article bemoans. *There is no discernable pattern to the chaos, no commonality,* it concludes.

All I know for certain is that I seem to be fading away.

Dr. Watt has closed his practice without notifying his patients. The doctor's odd choice of words suggest he has left the city with no forwarding address. The message on his machine confirming this was terse, asserting only *"my work here is done,"* whatever that means.

I don't even remember eating recently. I don't recall going to work, going out for anything, talking to my terrified neighbors, paying the bills. I no longer remember anything else concerning the mundane details of my work-a-day life, my leisure.

There is only this welcome, growing, inner peace enveloping me like an aura—a sense of hovering, weightlessness, no physicality; punctuated now and then by those inevitable headaches, the dizziness, the pimples, the suffocation, the blackouts, and those inexorable sirens in the night, growing ever more distant each time they respond.

Thomas Ligotti:
The Abyss of Radiance

S. C. Hickman

At this point it may seem that the consolations of horror are not what we thought they were, that all this time we've been keeping company with illusions. Well, we have. And we'll continue to do so, continue to seek the appalling scene which short-circuits our brain, continue to sit in our numb coziness with a book of terror on our laps like a cataleptic predator, and continue to draw smug solace, if only for the space of a story, from a world made snug and simple by absolute hopelessness and doom.

—Thomas Ligotti, *The Nightmare Factory*

I am no book thief. But I could not bear to part with your words...

> —Poppy Z. Brite, *On Thomas Ligotti*

Why do we read such works as these? A darkness unbearable, a world where nothing good ever happens, a realm of pure and unadulterated hopelessness and doom? Why? Even the notion that one could be consoled by such intemperate melodies of utter death and destruction, madness and delirium seem to send one back to that strange place of emptiness, that weird space of story where the thing we've been chasing, the object of horror that we've sought even against our own will (do we have a *will?*) suddenly stands revealed—not as a visible thing that we can observe, nor as a shaded emptiness that we can absolve into the particles of our mindless, aberrant fetish, obsess over, ponder as if it were the ultimate answer to our deepest longings; no, such are the illusory tricks of stagecraft magicians, no—what we seek is as in Walter Pater's aesthetic,

> A sudden light transfigures a trivial thing, a weather-vane, a windmill, a winnowing flail, the dust in the barn door; a moment - and the thing has vanished, because it was pure effect; but it leaves a relish behind it, a longing that the accident may happen again. [1]

It's this secret moment, this pure *effect:* a moment that cannot be shared, no testimony brought forth or enveloped with the reasoning powers of intellect; no, rather such moments that suddenly present their *absolute aura*—a profane light, a flame from

---

[1] Walter Pater. *The Renaissance: Studies in Art and Form.* (London and New York: MacMillan and Co., 1888), 185.

the darkness that attests not so much to our fear as to our exhilaration in the face of the unknown. Such moments leave us desperate, longing for the return, for the return of such infinitesimal mysteries, glints from elsewhere that awaken in us neither nostalgia nor some futurial glance into the mists of time forward; but, rather, give us hint of that seed that lies in the depths of our own mind as the outer form of some object breaks over us releasing powers we had as yet to register or distill from the voids surrounding us. For that is the key, we seek what cannot be locked down in the daylight of reason, a hint of that terror at the heart of the world which holds us in its desperate flight, if only momentarily a glance into the Real.

The Tsalal

A host of strangers come together at the intersection of time and space in a world between worlds. Their eyes "fixed with an insomniac's stare, the stigma of both monumental fatigue and painful attentiveness to everything in sight".[2] We are not given a reason, only that this gray host has returned to a place from which they were excluded. To what purpose if any have they returned? And, more to the point, why did they leave, abandon this place to begin with? A crime, an unimaginable collective massacre, some dark and unfathomable secret or burden to which staying meant certain madness and eventual death; or, was it just inexplicable, no reason at all, or one that they have long forgotten in their collective misery and spiritual ennui? A clue: "Only one had not gone with them. He had stayed in the skeleton town..."[3]

But why? Why would he stay and all the others leave, abandon

---

[2] Thomas Ligotti. *The Nightmare Factory* (Carroll & Graf), 1996.
[3] Ibid.

their homes (are they residents?) and depart to unknown lands or cities? Was there a natural or unnatural disaster? Something like those cities abandoned in Russia or America because of ecological and technological meltdown? A collective amnesia: "They were sure they had seen something they should not remember." [4] A murder, a sacrifice, a collective ritual of such magnitude and horror that they were all brought to that point of mental breakdown whose catastrophic consequence was some form of memory sickness and dementia: "A paralysis had seized them, that state of soul known to those who dwell on the highest plane of madness, aristocrats of insanity whose nightmares confront them on either side of sleep." [5] There is a sense of solidarity in madness, a hysterical craving after the truth of which they are both enamored and yet absolved to never discover again. And, yet, like one of Beckett's creatures in the hell of modernity: "I can't go on. I'll go on." This sense of being in-between, caught in the active and passive passage into the vastation of some banal *nihil*.

We know that for Thomas Ligotti there is a deeper truth unfolded in those darker thoughts of such thinkers as Schopenhauer, Eduard von Hartmann, Philipp Mainländer, Julius Bahnsen, Ernst Lindner, Lazar Hellenbach, Paul Deußen, Agnes Talbert, Olga Plümacher and, last but not least, the young Nietzsche. Something of the flavor of that spiritual anomie which gathers itself under the icon of pessimism. Those German Romantics, melancholy and suicidal—poet manqués who would define it as 'weltschmerze' ("worldpain") hinting at the dark moodiness of things whose aura was surrounded by sadness and

---

[4] Ibid.
[5] Ibid.

weariness weighing down the soul with an acute sense of evil and suffering at the heart of existence. As Fredrick C. Beiser will attest, "Its origins have been traced back to the 1830s, to the late romantic era, to the works of Jean Paul, Heinrich Heine..." and others.[6]

Yet, it was the Norwegian philosopher Peter Wessel Zapffe (1899– 1990), even more than the better-known Schopenhauer who would awaken in Ligotti the sense of utter futility and the dark contours of pessimism concerning the human condition and predicament:

> Nonhuman occupants of this planet are unaware of death. But we are susceptible to startling and dreadful thoughts, and we need some fabulous illusions to take our minds off them. For us, then, life is a confidence trick we must run on ourselves, hoping we do not catch on to any monkey business that would leave us stripped of our defense mechanisms and standing stark naked before the silent, staring void. To end this self-deception, to free our species of the paradoxical imperative to be and not to be conscious, our backs breaking by degrees upon a wheel of lies, *we must cease reproducing.*[7]

This notion of cessation, this withdrawal from the contract of organic *Will-to-live* in Schopenhauer's terms is the central motif of Zapffe's pessimism. Ligotti's, too. Yet, even in this strangest of tales, the stubborn refusal to die continues as if death were itself the very core of existence, a subtle circulation around a hollow abyss that could never find the flame that would end it all: "Blessed is the seed that is planted forever in darkness," a woman says. When asked what she meant by the invocation, she is as confused as the interlocutor.

---

[6] Frederick C. Beiser. Weltschmerz: Pessimism in German Philosophy, 1860-1900 (OUP Oxford; 1 edition April 28, 2016).

[7] Thomas Ligotti. *The Conspiracy against the Human Race: A Contrivance of Horror* (Hippocampus Press), June 23, 2012, 28-29.

Maybe that is how the outside circulates into our world, seeps into the daylight with its dark jets of inky delirium.

The Man Who Stayed Behind

Andrew Maness, like many of Ligotti's officiators, is a loner, a scholar or bookworm, and a misfit renegade from reality. As he stands in the room atop a mansion that once housed many of his predecessors, he watches these gray citizens wander the streets below him, each following some prerecorded script that even they do not understand but know they are powerless to abandon. In the room is a book that seems to hold both a secret and a mystery, one that Maness himself has sought to decipher for as long as he can remember: "You know what made them come home, but I can only guess. So many things you have devoutly embellished, yet you offer nothing on this point."[8] As if the book had a personality, as if it knew more than a book should know, a book that not only exceeded the limits of its covers but seemed to grow as the seed in the darkness grows. A book whose title would serve a greater mystery: TSALAL.

Many of Ligotti's tales speak of secret books whose forbidden knowledge reveals to its antagonists certain hellish paradises, utopian realms of utter, bittersweet *jouissance*: a jouissance which compels the subject to constantly attempt to transgress the prohibitions imposed on his enjoyment, to go beyond the pleasure principle (a la Lacan!). What Georges Bataille would speak of as "*the recoil imposed on everyone, in so far as it involves terrible promises...*"[9] Ligotti, as if in agreement, has always attributed to the (un)natural

---

[8] Thomas Ligotti. *The Nightmare Factory* (Carroll & Graf), 1996.
[9] Jacques Lacan, *The Four Fundamental Concepts of Psycho-Analysis,* W. W. Norton & Co Inc., 1st American Ed (September 1981), 234.

objects of his world—the mundane homes and streets of a village or city—this aura of terrible promise:

> Surrounding this area were clusters of houses that in the usual manner collect about the periphery of skeleton towns. These were structures of serene desolation that had settled into the orbit of a dead star. They were simple pinewood coffins, full of stillness, leaning upright against a silent sky. Yet it was this silence that allowed sounds from a fantastic distance to be carried into it. And the stillness of these houses and their narrow streets led the eye to places astonishingly remote. There were even moments when the entire veil of desolate serenity began to tremble with the tumbling colors of chaos.[10]

Most of Ligotti's most memorable passages are of night walks along the strange alleys, streets, and thoroughfares of certain villages and cities, where the imponderable strangeness of things seems to crawl down out of remote regions to merge and take up residence. This atmospheric prose-poetry is what unveils Ligotti's greatest strength rather than the narrative of the tales themselves. It's as if in such places there is a sense that the "magical desolation of narrow streets and coffin-shaped houses comes to settle and distill like an essence of the old alchemists."[11] In one of his better-known essays Walter Benjamin would speak of this as an *aura*:

> Historically, works of art had an 'aura' – an appearance of magical or supernatural force arising from their uniqueness (similar to mana). The aura includes a sensory experience of distance between the reader and the work of art. ... The aura has disappeared in the modern age because art has become reproducible.[12]

---

[10] Thomas Ligotti. *The Nightmare Factory* (Carroll & Graf), 1996.

[11] Ibid.

[12] Benjamin, Walter, *Illuminations: Essays and Reflections*, Ed. Hannah Arendt, Trans. Harry Zohn, New York: Schocken Books, 1968.

It's this sense of loss that pervades most of the stories in Ligotti's oeuvre. We sense this endless circling round the aura of an object that cannot be revealed without terrible consequence for both reader and author. To name it is to destroy it, so it remains outside in the dark, unnamed and full of that aura that against the modernists remain unreproducible. It cannot be profaned except on pain of death and annihilation.

Even as Andrew closes the book, the metamorphoses begin, a changing of shadow to shadow, an unfolding to an infernal paradise whose dark transports offer the reader neither comfort nor escape, consolation or reprieve. Andrew's father, a defender of day and light, a priest, whose dogmas seem out of another more medieval age reprimands his reprobate son:

> "There is nothing more awful and nothing more sinful than such changes in things. Nothing is more grotesque than these changes. All changes in things are grotesque. The very possibility of changes in things is grotesque. And the beast is the author of all changes. You must never again consort with the beast!"[13]

The orthodox seeks an unchanging world, a realm where time stands still and all things stave off the inevitable evil of change and movement. Andrew feels the burden of change growing in him, the "seed in the dark" growing.[14] It allures him and terrorizes him, and yet he knows it is his destiny. Like Adam in the garden, Andrew has been forced to renounce the temptation of his own fallen trees: forbidden books, the forbidden knowledge of those infernal regions

---

[13] Thomas Ligotti. *The Nightmare Factory* (Carroll & Graf), 1996.
[14] Ibid.

that offer and allure him toward the remote darkness. As his father says of these books: "I keep them…so that you may learn by your own will to renounce what is forbidden in whatever shape it may appear."[15]

Returning to that chapter in the Bible where the forbidden fruit of knowledge first offered its allurements, we find a serpent whispering in the woman's ear. The serpent is simply there, the tempter already in place, an unexplained occupant of the Garden—and of the human mind. The serpent appears to be the concentrated and symbolic remnant of an earlier religious age, before the Jews passed through the tumultuous shift from polytheism to monotheism. Nothing yet links the serpent to Satan/the Devil. It is calmly insubordinate and categorically denies God's verdict of death for eating the forbidden tree. "Thou shalt not surely die" (Genesis 3:4). The serpent tells the woman that, rather, the act will open their eyes and make them as gods. The woman eats and gives of the fruit to her husband. Everything goes by halves now. Adam and Eve start out innocent and immortal. The serpent claims that by eating the forbidden fruit, they will achieve divinity without losing immortality. He is half-right—that is, they attain insight into good and evil and at the same time they lose immortality. "And the Lord God said, Behold the man is become as one of us, to know good and evil: and now lest he put forth his hand, and take also of the tree of life, and eat, and live forever … the Lord God sent him forth from the garden of Eden" (Genesis 3:22). Because they have become mortal, Adam and Eve must now be kept away from the Tree of Life. Prohibition did not work for the first tree. Banishment is the

---

[15] Ibid.

logical answer.

This sense of prohibition and banishment or exclusion as the fruit of a temptation pervades many of Ligotti's stories. Breaking the prohibition often leads to utter madness and a break with the sane, everyday world of humanity, where the codes of sleep and blindness encode most humans in a dubious form of wakefulness. Yet, it is this very prohibition that awakens Andrew's desire: "But how wonderful he found those books that were forbidden to him." Or, again,

> He somehow knew these books were forbidden to him, even before the reverend had made this fact explicit to his son and caused the boy to feel ashamed of his *desire* to hold these books and to know their matter. He became bound to the worlds he imagined were revealed in the books, obsessed with what he conceived to be a cosmology of nightmares.[16]

Andrew would spend hours within this forbidden paradise of books and knowledge, mapping the underbelly of a universe that he could only see in his mind's eye. He imagined the stars in this private infernal universe: "They had changed in the strangest way, changed because everything in the universe was changing and could no longer be protected from the changes being worked upon them by something that had been awakened in the blackness, something that desired to remold everything it could see…and had the power to see all things."[17] This is a dark presence, a power of creativity and surprise that could suddenly remake the universe at will, an agent of change and metamorphosis such that in "those nights of dreaming, all things were subject to forces that knew nothing of law or reason,

---

[16] Ibid.
[17] Ibid.

and nothing possessed its own nature or essence but was only a mask upon the face of absolute darkness, a blackness no one had ever seen."[18]

Ultimately even these forbidden books offered little consolation to Andrew. What he sought was another book, access to a forbidden knowledge that seemed to offer,

> …a counter-creation, and the books on the shelves of his father's library could not reveal to him what he desired to know of this other genesis. While denying it to his father, and often to himself, he dreamed of reading the book that was truly forbidden, the scripture of a deadly creation, one that would tell the tale of the universe in its purest sense.[19]

Andrew remonstrates his father over the hideousness of these prohibitory measures, arguing that all they did was cause the very thing his father sought to end — the desire for a forbidden knowledge of things that no book held or could hold but the one whose very temptation was bound to the darkness of his own mind and nightmares:

> You preached to me that all change is grotesque, that the very possibility of change is evil. Yet in the book you declare 'transformation as the only truth'— the only truth of the Tsalal, that one who is without law or reason. 'There is no nature to things,' you wrote in the book. 'There are no faces except masks held tight against the pitching chaos behind them.' You wrote that there is not true growth or evolution in the life of this world but only transformations of appearance, an incessant melting and molding of surfaces without underlying essence. Above all you pronounced that there is no salvation of any being because no beings exist as such, nothing exists to be saved—everything,

---

[18] Ibid.
[19] Ibid.

everyone exists only to be drawn into the slow and endless swirling of mutations that we may see every second of our lives if we simply gaze through the eyes of the Tsalal. [20]

It's this sense of a counter-world, not a mirror world but a realm that is counter-factual and disturbs, even intrudes our own world; a world that is already seeping into ours from remote dimensions that is at the heart of Ligotti's works. As if all along this very realm we are in is that eternally metamorphosing, infernal region of change, but that through the secret wizardry of those dark agents of time, the time of change was stopped, and that we've all been imprisoned in a lifeless universe of the death-drive, pursuing a circular and repetitive course of unchanging repetition. Isn't this the dream of those oligarchs of thought surrounding us inside a world of capitalistic desire, a realm in which the only circulation is that of immaterial goods and money, a realm where nothing changes so much as the static representation of change — a change that is itself a repetition of death?

Maybe in the end we—all of us—are Andrew awakening to the truth, a truth he comes to see as the horror of his and our unchanging society. As he says to his father: "You knew this was the wrong place when you brought me here as a child. And I knew that this was the wrong place when I came home to this town and stayed here until everyone knew that I had stayed too long in this place." [21]

We all know this is the truth, that we've allowed this world to continue down its unnatural course, allowed leaders to lead us nowhere and nowhen—a circular void of capitalist desire in a

---

[20] Ibid.
[21] Ibid.

vacuum of consuming consummation; a realm where time and space have accelerated into a virtual hellhole of circulating capital to which we are all bound like cogs in a vast machinic system. Knowing what we know, we still desire it: and, that is our burden and our downfall. And, yet, we all have known for a long while that the forbidden knowledge that would free us of this trap has been in plain sight all along, our eyes glued to its strange temptations: the eyes of the Tsalal. Shall we open those eyes, now, and begin to change, metamorphosize beyond this seeming world of stasis and repetition? As we open our eyes the infernal seeps in... the dark seed sprouts...

In the ancient Gnostic Gospels of Valentinus, there is a back and forth between the Pleroma ("Place of Fullness") and the Abyss ("Place of Emptiness"), in which a dialectical interaction transpires between the powers of fullness and absence, an oscillation and hesitation between the visible darkness and the darkness made visible, a seeming that stages a cosmic battle and forces that which cannot be named to give birth to the dark seed: the parental abyss, at once foremother and forefather, from which the babe rushes forth into our emptiness. And, we, like the cannibalistic villagers of Ligotti's "The Tsalal," must consume the fleshy remains of such corruption, become one with its energetic will, and let the white bones sink into black earth where in the darkness a light will begin to shine: a nihilistic light, glimmers of strange wonders filtering up from the radiant Abyss.

Ligotti, a subtle master of the unsaid, never exposes the reality below the surface edge of his prose-poetry. Rather, he hints at it, allowing the reader to intermingle in the shifting sands of the tale's infernal paradise, whereby either the dark seed of its intent will awaken in her the mystery from elsewhere; else, close the portal forever into this dark realm, leaving the reader only a momentary gleam, an impossible enchantment, subtly trapping her in her own allurements.

Bibliography

Beiser, Frederick C. Weltschmerz: *Pessimism in German Philosophy, 1860-1900*. OUP: Oxford; 1 edition, April 28, 2016.

Benjamin, Walter, *Illuminations: Essays and Reflections*, Ed. Hannah Arendt, Trans. Harry Zohn, New York: Schocken Books, 1968.

Lacan, Jacques, *The Four Fundamental Concepts of Psycho-Analysis*. W. W. Norton & Co Inc.: 1st American edition, September 1981.

Ligotti, Thomas. *The Conspiracy against the Human Race: A Contrivance of Horror*. Hippocampus Press: June 23, 2012.

—. *The Nightmare Factory*. Carroll & Graf., June 27, 1996.

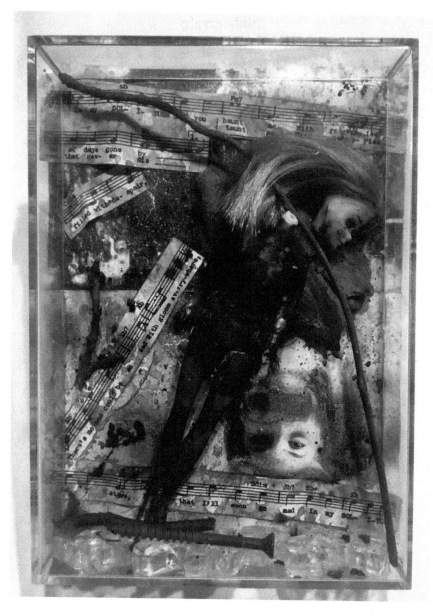

Haunted
Danielle Hark

The Milk Man

Alana I. Capria

I COMMITTED US to the spilled milk, wrote our names in the curdling: ME, MILK MAN. I pricked my fingers—pinky for the womb demon, ring finger for the blood angel, middle finger for the cunt goddess, pointer finger for the aborted seraphim, thumb for the miscarriage nymph—and dripped red into the white. Once the milk puddles were marbled with my blood, I skimmed the mixture into my mouth. The milk tasted terrible—like vomit, old cum—but I needed to swallow it all for the ritual to work. It needed to be blood and milk, taken deep inside my body, so that the milk man was stitched tight to me. I swallowed until my spoon scraped the floor, then I licked the milk directly from the tiles. The rancid taste triggered my gag reflex; my insides heaved against these mouthfuls, shouted NO. NO. But it was done, the floor cleaned of milk, my pricked fingers clotting. I sat naked on a milk crate and thought solely of the milk man. I thought of his face for many hours, until the refrigerator light bulb burned out, then I thought of his face in the dark, the brown of his eyes, the stubble of his face. I thought of him until I was no longer certain it was his face I imagined; even thinking seemed a trick. Then I could not think of the milk man anymore and simply sat in the cold...

A little bit of the milk man remained in the refrigerator with me. It pressed against me as I sat, breathed so that I heard his voice in my ear. There were many instances in which I considered ending the ritual, moving on to another man, but the milk man's presence motivated me to continue. Each day was long with blood and milk and nudity. I numbed around my hips, my hair fell out. These curls floated in the milk spills; I pulled them up and knotted them around my fingers (it was not long before they loosened and fell). I thought of the milk man, whispered his name until that was the only sound my mouth could make, repeated his name in my sleep. I thought only of him, with such fervor and reverence that it was like speaking of a god. As I thought of him, a smaller part of me said: He will kill me. Another part said: Perhaps he will not. Another part said: It will be like death but also not. Then those parts were silent, and I said his name louder. And still he was not here, not yet, not for some time. The blood went brown, the milk puddles dried, and eventually, I donned a blanket, and later, a coat...

The bloody milk did its job. The milk man came back. I heard his milk truck, and then there he was, pushing me down against the milk crates. My fingers still ached from the bloodletting, yet I coaxed him into my hands, stroked until he finished. The milk man grabbed me by the cunt, breasts, throat. I bruised beneath his hands, and he gripped me harder, nearly ripping chunks of flesh from me. I smelled blood, I tasted milk. The refrigerator light blinked on and off. I saw the milk man, then I did not. This went on and on and on. I felt a crumbling in my stomach and knew it to be something like a demon settling down within me. My ribs were too confining, my bones too hard, my ligaments too leathered, my fat too thick. Did this entity belong to the man or me? It lived inside my skin; perhaps that meant it was solely mine. I worried that this presence might turn the milk man away; he might leave me alone in the refrigerator. I saw him eyeing the door and felt another crumbling, one that nearly dropped me to my knees. Then I imagined a little voice trilling behind my breastbone: Woman, there are many other ways...

I needed the milk man to always think of me, so I made him dream. It was not so difficult: I spat in his mouth, then closed my eyes. That night, he dreamed I coiled around his throat like a snake, squeezing until his bones cracked. The next night, he dreamed he swallowed me dozens of times, just gulp, gulp, gulp. The night after, he dreamed that I nestled deep inside his body, breathing through his lungs. Then he dreamed I lay naked at the center of a spider's web with him at my feet, his body encased in silk. The night after, he dreamed he and I were alone in a dark room. Then he dreamed I opened my stomach to him. Then he dreamed I lay upon a grill and he ate directly from my ribs. Then he dreamed I brought my slit wrists to his face and soaked him with my blood. Then he dreamed he weeded a garden and each weed had a bulb at the end that looked so much like me. Then he dreamed he was dead, blind, and mute, yet a voice came resounding through his head and that voice was mine. Then he dreamed that I swam through a tub of foamy milk.

Then he dreamed of me and dreamed of me and dreamed of me. In those final dreams, I sat on an ashen wood floor and smiled at him. When the milk man woke, he pressed me against the wall and possessed me completely. I protested half-heartedly (I wanted to hurt him then) but felt a rumbling in my gut that quieted me. This rumbling was like hunger but also not. I was confused and stayed quiet until it passed...

To keep the milk man, he needed a piece of me. I examined my naked flesh, choosing the perfect slab for him. Some flesh was too milky, other flesh too dark. Some flesh was too wrinkled, some too smooth. Some had hair, others no pores. On the inside of my left thigh, I found the perfect patch: soft and golden and lightly veined. I cut it from myself, sliced in a circle until the meat was freed. I kissed this meat and my lips were stained. I offered the milk man this meat cradled in my palms. He stared at this meat for too long, then knocked it to the floor. It is old meat, he said. I am younger than you, I said. It is still old, he said. It is aged, used, marked. I went to where the meat dropped on the floor. I turned it over, saw how right he was, how the flesh was more mottled than I realized, how the veins were closer to the surface, the raw meat on the underside purple instead of red. I saw how the milk man believed this meat an insult, and so I gobbled it up so that it was away from him. The meat was sour on my tongue, but I chewed and chewed. The open wound on my thigh bled freely. The refrigerator smelled of old milk and fresh blood. The milk man passed me, and the smell came from him, too...

My skin bruised, swelled with sub-dermal bleeding. I took pins to these swellings so that I might milk the blood out. The blood was milky, swirled with thin whiteness. I collected the drippings in a small cup that I kept in a corner of the refrigerator. These drippings congealed into a custard that the milk man and I later shared. We fed one another tiny spoonfuls, the blood pudding so concentrated, our tongues hurt from the taste. The milk man refused every bite I offered, only swallowed when I forced the spoon between his lips. When he fed me, I moaned with displeasure, the blood strange despite being my own. I imagined my veins, all those long ropes yanked free of my body, tossed like a net to the floor. I imagined taking scissors to that netting, cutting it open, leaving it as a trap upon the tiles. In that netting, I might catch the milk man and if not him, then another like him. Eventually, I might have a collection of milk men, each more troubled than the last but with a larger cock. This thought delighted me, and so I ate the remainder of the blood pudding, then tossed the empty cup to the back of the refrigerator where it rolled beneath a shelf and was lost forever. The milk man paced around me. He went to the refrigerator door, touched the knob, returned. He touched every stacked milk crate, cradled those that lay loose on the floor. I knew there was another place he wished to be, a place far from this refrigerator, a place that did not smell like sour milk. And still I kept him here, selfishly and with great delight...

But I was not happy. The milk man did not look at me the way I wanted. The dreams were not enough. He was no longer affected by the bloody milk. He retreated from me, took away his tower of milk crates, found the ones I kept in hiding, took them as well. I felt disemboweled when I saw the crates were no longer where I left them. I felt a physical gaping, a tearing down my middle. I thought I might die. I could only wait for the milk man to reappear, to grab me by the throat and squeeze until I saw red. I waited impatiently, my bones grating, my skin crawling, but he did not come. Other milk men came, ugly men who were no longer young. I did not let these men near me; I demanded the first milk man. I refused the milk, pushed the crates over. These men all retreated, and when there were no milk men left, my milk man was forced to return. He came to me with a broken bottom lip. His blood trickled slowly, and I licked the wound, drew his wounded lip into my mouth, sucked until no more blood came from him. I sat back on my heels, the taste of him fading from my tongue. Do you love me? the milk man asked. I thought I might vomit with glee. Of course not, I said...

Soon, it all worsened. I felt myself withering. This withering happened slowly, first around my fingernails, then the corners of my bottom lip. I felt it behind my eyelids, then at the back of my neck. It was at the roof of my mouth, in the middle of my throat, around my left nipple. I noticed it on my right wrist, just above my left knee, in a patch around my right ankle, inside my belly button. What is this, I said, but I already knew. It was because of the milk man. He leeched from me, sucking my flesh until the moisture was gone. This withering was because the milk man was all I thought of. I dreamed of him, wrote his name on the insides of my thighs, drank milk while thinking hard on him. I did not want this to be; withering very quickly led to death. And so, I thought of a ritual, that I might stave off this rotting. When the milk man was not looking, I crept behind him and cut the back of his neck. I only needed a few drops of his blood and so the cut was very small, just a prick. With his blood upon my knife, I slashed lightly across my left knee and so our bloods swirled together. I licked the knife clean, chased the red with a glass of fresh milk (it still tasted sour), then slept while the milk man groped me. I felt him vaguely, as though I was outside my body, and so slept on, without stirring, allowing time for the hex placed upon me to drain onto the floor. When I finally woke, I saw a black smear near the floor drain. It was like mold but wetter, and I was so glad to see all this filthiness finally gone from me...

And still, despite the black residue being emptied from my body, the withering continued. It slowed when the milk man was near, worsened when he went away. I was consumed by thoughts of him. I suffered diarrhea for several days, my body incapable of fully digesting anything I ate. It all ran through me. I dehydrated, and my stomach cramped. There was nothing I could do. I wanted to drink the milk, but it was what made me sick. Each mouthful was harsh, but I still swallowed. I drank gallon after gallon, pricked my fingers, dripped the blood into each full bottle. I drank potion and spell, ritual and sacrament. I thought: Milk man, milk man, milk man. I smelled sour and blood. I sobbed in the bathroom as my body ran out into the drain. I said: Milk man, milk man, milk man. I lay on the refrigerator floor with the emptied crates stacked around me. I looked through their holes, imagined myself in a prison made of black plastic. Milk man, milk man, milk man, I whispered. I bit my tongue, but the pain only made the milk man's name more alluring. Soon, I had a knife in my hand. Soon, the knife was against my knees. Soon, I was cutting, sawing away. Soon, my legs were red with blood. I drank milk as the blood dried brown. I drank milk while picking the scabs. I stuffed those scabs into the few milk gallons I had left. There, they softened, infused the milk with their bloodiness. I drank the milk later, thinking only of the milk man, and that was when he returned, his own fingers bloodied and the unsavory smell of refuse in his pores...

I was better than this. The milk man was only a milk man. I thought of that little voice inside me, and I knew that hidden within myself was a beastly woman who was rooted to my womb. She peered out the thin skin of my throat. She clung to the root of my tongue and made me say the words she wanted. She felt very large, and I choked upon her. She was mine. I trusted her in the way I did not trust the milk man. I withered, and this beastly woman grew stronger. She said: Eat him up. Bones and hair and gristle and all. Leave nothing, not a scab. She starved for the milk man, was desperate to swallow him down. She sniffed his neck, gnashed her teeth because I did not bite. This beastly woman bleated like a goat, ripped at my stomach, made my sickness worse. Eat, she shouted. Eat! But how could I? If I ate the milk man up, then he would be gone, and I would be alone. I drank milk to silence my beastly woman. I filled my gut, lay on my side with my belly swelled. My beastly woman ranted and raved. She clawed at me in a frenzy, tore up my insides, shredded my entrails to rags. The milk man came close and the beastly woman heaved. I did not look at him, I could not. I am pregnant, I said. It is not mine, the milk man said. What will we do? I asked. Be a husband and wife, the milk man said. And my beastly woman crept out of me, licked her teeth, and said: No, no, that will not do...

The Unraveling
Tatiana Garmendia

Trans Woman Gutted

Valin Paige

i think i would like my body
to come to an end somewhere
along a stretch of roasting
Oklahoma highway

drops of blood evaporate into
a thick kind of pudding against
bow leggedness
splayed out as unfortunate
deer leaping at just
the wrongest moment

rib & hip tips pointing up &
up as the sky balloons
into a new kind of night

soft on dust wind

i would like it to be during
crow hunting season
when they are most scared
of being shot for their
hunger

did you know Oklahoma allows
crow hunting
& there is no bag
limit on crows
burlap can be heavy & dark & full
of thick beaks & bead eyes twitching

i think i would like to end
as a crow's last meal
there seems something
right in that
a lack of hunting limits

& a scrapping of warm
insides
against a thing's hard
wanted beak

Silhouette
Danielle Hark

What Found Nevaeh

Donyae Coles

"ZION DIED," MRS. Porter said from down the hall, halting Nevaeh's hand, the key centimeters from the lock. The light above Mrs. Porter flickered, off, on, off, on casting her dark, wrinkled face into darkness and then murky shadows. Never real light. The woman almost disappeared into the piss yellow hallway, a phantom wrapped in a faded housecoat that may have been blue once but had turned into a sad gray. Gray sock covered feet stuffed into ratty slippers, one thin hand scratching at her sagging cheek before moving to worry at her snow-white hair, the brightest thing in the hall. Neveah thought one day she would look like that, would be lucky to look like that one day because it meant she made it, she survived.

She turned glaucoma milky eyes to Neveah. "That you

Neveah?"

"Yeah Mrs. Porter, yeah it's me. Sorry to hear about Zion. I'll try to check in with his people."

The old woman nodded, jowls bouncing with each movement of her head. "Good you came home, not safe out there. It's a mess, a mess, that poor boy. Wasn't like this when I was young. Wasn't like this at all. Poor boy, poor boy. A mess."

"Uh-huh," Nevaeh replied, her head mimicking the woman's nods. The light flickered off-on-off-on, and she noticed something different about the hall in each shift. A cracked floor tile, the wet gleam of Mrs. Porter's wedding ring, a water stain on the ceiling, the thick, blue veins that peeked out above Mrs. Porter's socks, a dark smudge that looked like oil on the wall. Things she must have seen a thousand, a million times before, anything not to look at the woman's face more, her mouth with its too white false teeth, her pale, nearly unseeing eyes. Anything not to be reminded that she would be lucky to be her one day. The light flickered like breaths, Mrs. Porter's speech a heartbeat—no longer words—only a rhythm.

Neveah's eyes flitted back to the patch of oil on the wall, focused, tried to break the spell, but it pulsed in time with the light. Off-on-off-on. A trick of the flicker, it grew with each pulse, spilling off the edges of reality and filling the wall as she stared and nodded. "Uh-huh, uh-huh," her own dull breath as the oil slick spread, a darkness that wasn't really darkness, a trick of the light, slithered along cracks and breaks in the wall and floor.

"He was about your age, wasn't he?" Mrs. Porter asked suddenly.

She pulled her eyes away from the spot. "What? Umm, no, I'm older than him, I think? He just graduated high school. I'm almost 30."

The old woman nodded, her head bobbing. "Of course, how silly of me. You get to be my age, though, seen all what I seen, and a baby is a baby. You all babies. Just babies. A mess."

Neveah smiled and nodded, eager to be done, eager to get out of the hallway, a dull ache boiling in the back of her head, the piss color of the hall slowly brightening but looking no less like urine. Off-on-off-on. "I've gotta get inside and start dinner," Neveah said, pushing to end things.

"You got kids? You don't got kids," the woman said. "I'd remember."

"No, I don't have any, but I have to work early tomorrow, need to get to bed," she replied.

The old woman seemed to accept that and nodded. "Of course, of course. Don't forget to check in with Zion's mama. A mess, just a mess."

Neveah didn't respond. Instead, she slipped the key into the lock and turned it, the motion smooth and easy. For a moment she thought her door wouldn't open; then that it would open but that inky blackness would be there, pressing through the opening and out into the hall to meet its fellow. The door swung open to nothing, just her empty apartment. The empty, still darkness.

"I'll talk to you later, Mrs. Porter," she said, inching past the doorway.

"They opened the laundry room again," the old woman replied, the announcement just as stark as the one she had made for Zion's death.

"We have a laundry room?" Neveah asked.

"Uh-huh, been closed up for years, but the new owners, they

fixed it up. Maybe they'll fix up the lights up here too. Too much for me. I can't do all them stairs, and they haven't gotten around to the elevator."

She nodded, "I'll check it out."

The old woman nodded in return, finally turning her eyes away from Neveah. *You'll be lucky,* she thought to herself as the woman turned, turned, turned, heading back into her own apartment, leaving Neveah alone with nothing but the oil slick and water stains and the piss yellow hallway, the light flickering off, on, off, on.

She shook her head and slid into her own apartment, shutting the door, locking it behind her. She breathed in the familiar scent, navigating the landscape in the dark. Inside her apartment, shaggy and inherited, the old furniture from before still there, left over from her uncle who had passed but put her name on the lease before he did so. A cheat that afforded her the two-bedroom apartment in exchange for a year of her life, a year of caring, a year off so he, her uncle, could die comfortably. He owed her at least that. She didn't like to think of the why, just that she had made it, had gotten what was owed her, that she survived. The chair where he had taken his last hacking breaths while she made coffee in the kitchen still sat in the living room, the seat indented, waiting for a body that would never return to it. The medical equipment had been removed at least. She couldn't stand that in the apartment. Given away to neighbors who needed it. Some old and tired. Some just tired. It didn't matter the reason, Neveah was happy to be rid of it all, but the chair stayed.

And she stayed.

In the dark, she moved around the old recliner and into the

kitchen, dropping her purse on the counter and pacing back to the bathroom. She turned on the light, click, on, and the dingy tile met her, yellow under the bulb. She pulled her work pants down and sat, kicking them the rest of the way off as she sat on the pot. Finished, she washed her hands while she stared at her face in the mirror. Dark bags under her dark eyes that stared out of her dark face, surrounded by her dark locks. No trick of the light, just her.

But there, behind her, on the wall, a stain. She turned to it, a spreading stain on the wall. Irregular in the way that dough or putty was irregular when you slammed it on the table and rolled it out. No mark of dripping. It didn't look as though something were leaking behind the plaster or cement or whatever made the building. She peered closer, wondering at the shape, as if someone had pressed something wet there, and it left a mark but too dark to be water.

She touched it, just the barest brush of her finger, expecting it to come up slippery with oil. Dry, her finger, the wall. Still it looked wet. Shiny but not water.

Was someone here, a workman? she wondered, looking around the small space thinking it may be paint or some fixative they had left smeared, but nothing seemed repaired. They could do that, just come in when they wanted, no notice. She knew from the lease she had skimmed before she signed it, hastily, ready to agree to anything just to have that break. But in all that time, they, the landlords, those mysterious owners, hadn't passed the threshold. Hadn't repaired a single thing. Now was no different. The toilet still ran, the shower still leaked slowly, slowly leaving the air damp and noisy at all times.

Shaking her head, she turned away, left the bathroom and started on her dinner. She turned on lights, the TV, used the pots and pans her uncle had left with the food she had brought. Ate it from his plates with her own fork before showering only to find that she had run out of clean panties.

She frowned at the laundry pile, then checked the time. *Still early,* she thought. Enough time to wash clothes and still get some sleep. "Oh, I can go to the basement, check that out," she hummed. She dug through the pile, pulling out a few items and dropping them into a laundry bag. She dressed in loose sweats and tennis shoes. She gathered her keys, dropping them in her pocket, and the half full bottle of laundry detergent. Settled, she opened her door.

She stepped into the hall, half-expected Mrs. Porter to still be standing there at the door, staring at nothing, waiting to tell her that Zion had died or some other ill omen with her too bright teeth and too thin hands. *I'd be lucky,* she thought briefly before shaking the words away. The light flickered. Off-on-off-on, and her eyes caught the stain, the oil slick, again. The one in the hall larger than the one in her bathroom. It pulsed.

I'm tired, she thought shaking her head, turning away and back down the stairs that led to the basement.

"You hear about Zion? That boy from 4B? Say he got shot. Shame," a voice said, the woman's words carried through the hall and down the stairs. Everything carried in the building, though. In her own apartment, she could hear Mrs. Porter coughing throughout the night. She wondered, sometimes, if Mrs. Porter had heard her uncle, had known what his death sounded like. It had sounded so plain to her as she sipped a cup of coffee and watched him struggle. So much like a normal cough. Wet but normal. She knew what it was, knew that the sound was off in a way she couldn't describe. She waited until she had finished her coffee to call the paramedics.

"They know who did it?" a second voice as she made her way down the steps.

The first person snorted, a dismissive sound, "Heard it was the cops but heard it was the other boy he was fighting with too. Heard a lot of shit. But so soon after little Rosita? And what was that other? The OD?"

Out of earshot, now she descended, trying to picture him now. *Zion,* she thought, *was he in high school or just young? Am I thinking of the right person?* She tried to remember who lived on the fourth floor, one above her, and came up with the barest ideas. She knew there were children from the stopping of feet she heard above her, the cartoons on too loud. She knew there was an older couple too because they had gotten some of her uncle's equipment. She thought she remembered a teenager with golden skin and a sweet smile under a high fade. But there was no way to know. Maybe he was the son, or maybe he was the man she sometimes heard yelling through the ceiling. Maybe Zion wasn't a teenager at all.

Ground floor, she paused at the door, a streetlight shown through the door, filling it with light. The same yellow tiles, cracked and broken as they were on her floor and there, under the mailboxes, that oil stain. *Something is leaking, mold probably. What a hassle for the new owners,* she shook her head as she turned away, moving towards the last set of stairs that led to the basement.

She didn't bother to peer into the glass portion of the door; she bumped it open with her body. The safety lights flickered above her as the one in her hall had before. Off-on-off-on as she took the steps, quickly, the halls silent. The walls she passed dotted with that strange oil, that slick, that had followed her down the stairs, had found its way into her apartment. *Mold.* She shook her head, *had to be*, but it was fine, worth the price to have the place locked in. She was, in that way, lucky. *I shoulda asked*, she realized as she approached the second set of doors. There would be storage, some of it hers, but she had never been. Whatever waited there was her uncle's, and she had no stomach for cleaning it out, and somewhere in that great basement expanse would be the mythical laundry room.

She pushed open the door and the stale air of storage met her. Locked shelves full of boxes and bric-a-brac lined the walls and just past them another light. Bright and new, like nothing else in the building had ever been. Brighter even than the streetlight that had spilled in from outside.

She stepped towards it, her feet dragging her through the room, but a sense of not quite dread filled her. Every step that drew her forward settled something just a little off in some part of her. She felt a beacon in her primal mind, in her belly. The lights flickered, off-on-off-on, and played their tricks, making that bright white space ahead seem to breathe. To expand and contract in time, but still she moved forward.

It's quiet down here, she thought, eyes cutting from side to side as she gripped her detergent in one sweaty hand, her laundry clutched in the other, but she couldn't stop, couldn't hold on to the silence as she moved forward, her feet carrying her over the threshold and into the newly painted, newly lit space beyond.

She stumbled and sucked in a gasping breath, not even aware that she had been holding it for the long walk from the steps into all this light, all this newness.

Stretched before her were the washers on one side, the dryers on the other. *Just like the cages, shelves,* she thought, shaking her head. Now here in the room she could hear them as they spun and went about their work. A small laugh escaped her throat. *Sound is so weird in this building,* she thought as she made her way down the line to the first empty washer she found.

"Fuck, coin-operated," she cursed, her pockets empty, save for her keys.

"Need some change?"

She turned to the sound of the deep voice, deep but young. Behind her, leaning against the washers, stood a boy just on the cusp of manhood or maybe a man just out of boyhood. She couldn't tell. He had eyes like oil, his hair twisted in the beginning of dreads. He crossed his arms over his chest, and his face held an amused smile. *He's so bright,* she thought, confused by the words.

"I didn't bring my wallet," she said.

He laughed, a rich sound, but there was something off, something she couldn't quite pinpoint. "I'm just playing. Don't worry about it. They haven't got around to fixing it all the way. You know, they work, but you don't gotta pay yet."

"It doesn't seem like the owners would be ok with people using them then," she said slowly.

He shrugged, "Don't matter. You'll pay eventually. Might as well take advantage while we can."

"Yeah, fuck them, bout time they fixed something around here."

The boy-man-man-boy smiled at her, showing off white teeth, "Need help?"

His words had a ring she understood, and for a second, a small blip in time, she considered them. But no, no, not her, not him. There were too many uncertainties, and she wasn't HIM. Wasn't like him at all. Didn't even want to chance it. He was too unknown.

She smiled, "No, I can handle my own laundry."

"Suit yourself. It's up to you. It's always up to you."

He turned to the dryer, and she turned to the washer, opening the door into a void, an oil slick black hole, she jumped back, expecting to bump into him but she met air. Turning, she found herself alone, and the pristine wall above the dryers now held one odd shaped black stain, an oil slick and no boy-man-man-boy. She sucked in a deep breath.

"Where?" she asked the empty air, the sound of the washers and dryers like breathing. She turned back to the way she had come, but she couldn't see through the flickering light. *He just left. I'm tired,* she thought to herself as she turned back to the machine to find nothing but an empty washer.

She loaded her laundry and added the soap. As he had said, the dials worked just fine, no change needed. Exhaling, she smiled and stepped back, watching the machine fill up. *Should I wait?* she thought, staring at the window where her clothes waited for water.

No water came, though. The space before her turned black with something heavier, thicker than water. "Oh, no!" she jumped forward and pulled the door open, and the liquid spilled onto the floor, just missing her shoes but not splashing. Whatever that heavy liquid was, it poured and pooled from the washer to her feet. She backed up to the dryers, but their motion pushed her forward, back to the mouth of the machine.

Down the row, more poured out, collecting on the smooth floor, puddling and pooling towards her in a steady slide.

That part of her that had hummed before, whispering that something was off, screamed now, it howled in her gut and her head, forcing her body to act, to *move*. Her arms went first, heavy and slow, as if what was on the floor had already gotten her, and then her legs, leaden, dragged themselves into motion, and suddenly she moved, out of the pristine laundry room that slowly filled with black and into the flickering lights of the storage, but here too things had changed.

No longer were the shelves stacked neatly against the walls. No, these cages formed a maze on the floor. A simple maze made of the unneeded belongings of all her neighbors. "What?" she half shouted as she slammed into the first. A simple puzzle that her panicked mind could not readily solve, instead she followed the only instinct she had and ran, dragging her hands along the cages, using touch to find an exit as the liquid poured behind her.

Feather-light touches met her at each brush of her fingers as deeper into the maze she moved. Soon the cages rattled back at her and she saw, clearly saw, eyes, small and quick in their depths among the Christmas decorations and old sports equipment.

Fingers and mouths touched her hands, her own digits tangling in hair as she passed. The light flickered above her, obscuring the figures in the cages. She wanted to pull away, wanted to stop touching but she couldn't any more than she could stop running, stop following the twisting path that the cages made for her. She couldn't see, not as she ran past and couldn't spare the time to turn, not when she needed to get out.

She could feel it licking at her heels the way the things, the people, their memories, the things in the cages licked at her fingers, tasting her. She rounded the corner, throwing herself forward to where she thought the door should be, but there stood only another cage.

"Fuck, no, no, no," she yelled and tried to push it, but it

wouldn't budge. Immovable, it stood, blocking her way. She pulled at the door, glancing back at the slow crawl of the liquid, the cages that shuddered in the half-darkness.

Breathless, she turned back to the cage that blocked the door and saw the edge of a bright pink jacket. *That's mine,* she thought frantically. *From that summer when I was nine. I lost it at my aunt's. I was playing with my uncle and I lost,* her mind shut like a trap on the memory, but it didn't matter, the rest she knew was true. *I can go through, I can go through,* she repeated, the mantra born from the place in her that could taste the offness of the world around her. The place that woke up after she lost her jacket and a whole lot more, but it didn't matter right now. Off didn't matter. Out mattered.

She scrambled for her keys and in shaky fingers located the never used one, the small one she had been given before her uncle died hacking in his chair while she smiled. The oil, thick and perfectly dark, reached her sneakers as she slid the key into the lock, pooled as she turned the lock and flung open the door.

Inside there was light, bright light that poured from an opening that seemed to breathe in time with her own body. *Off,* she thought briefly but threw herself into the light.

It crushed her, sliding, unseen hands over a body that didn't feel exactly like hers but one she remembered. Smaller and unready for such acts, she didn't scream as she hadn't screamed then. All of it familiar, she pushed through, her mind as bright and blank as the world that was not a world around her. When it felt as if it couldn't crush her anymore, she slid free from it whole and grown.

She stumbled on the ground, cold air filling her lungs.

"You ok, sis?" a familiar voice said, and she felt a hand on her shoulder. She looked up. The boy-man-man-boy stared at her, his oil black eyes soft, all pupil, he blinked, and they turned black. He smiled and blinked again, drawing tears, thick and dark that tumbled down his cheeks. "S'not so bad now that you know, right? Now that the price's been paid for it, s'not so bad."

She stood straight, "Who are you? What's happening?"

"Zion," he said, pointing to his chest, just over his heart before he shrugged. "We've got new owners and rent's due."

He walked backwards as the world moved in reverse for a moment until he stood, arm raised in front of another young man, poised to strike, the world held still before it crashed back to life with his fist impacting the other's face, slamming him into the ground.

Someone shouted, words she couldn't catch and shots like the world cracking open filled the air. One ripped into Zion, and he turned with the impact, a red bloom upon his chest where he had pointed before. He fell to his knees, and she saw his eyes, not pools of oil but brown, brown like coffee before he fell, face first to the ground. The world cracked again, and she ran to the entrance of her building, pushing open the door and stumbled into her own hallway but it was off. The angles of it weren't right, the flickering, the off-on-off-on off rhythm, *The breathing,* she thought, looking at the walls that seemed more pus than piss now.

She fell to the floor, the cracked tile buckling gently with the pressure of the oil that pulsed in that same off pattern as the light. She stood up and looked down the hall. There stood Mrs. Porter, her back to Nevaeh, and she stared at the oil spot on the wall, grown huge and heavy as it pressed against the wall, the reality of things. Between the old woman's legs something wet and bright collected.

"I heard," the woman said from down the hall. "I heard, and I knew, but it was fine, fine. He was due. And so were you. Zion died. Did you see his people? Just upstairs."

"Uh-huh, I'm going to go, just gotta change my clothes, ok?" She inched to the door. She didn't want the old woman to turn. A part of her screamed *off*, knew that she couldn't bear to see the woman's face, that it wouldn't be a face when she turned. That it would be just one milky eye weeping, wetting the front of her.

"That's fine, dear, they're waiting for you. His people. The new owners. They're all waiting for you. You're due."

Nevaeh moved slowly, grasping her doorknob. She had lost her keys in the basement, but it didn't matter. The door swung open, and she stepped forward into a cold afternoon.

She turned to see herself, frozen, smiling gently with a cup of coffee. No uncle filled the indention on the recliner. No tampered with medical equipment either. The form of a man sat there but all inky. A wet void.

It stared at her, she could feel that, the heaviness. The part of her that knew *off* knew this too. That she was due. Owed or past due didn't matter, the time to settle was before her as it was before Mrs. Porter, as it had been for Zion and maybe for Rosita and the person who OD'ed. Maybe for everyone.

The oil, wet and slick, rippled, and she saw it, the depths of the horror, the unfathomable *offness* of it all that felt almost like her real life. The same fears, the same despair. But then something else, a light like she had never seen, and that part of her that knew *off* hummed in something like pleasure but greater, so much greater. Something she hadn't felt for years, hadn't known she could feel anymore at all. Something she thought she lost with her jacket.

"I can leave, I can go upstairs. I can go out the window," she said, and the slick in front of her did not respond. "I'm lucky, I get this. The choice is mine."

It stood, it expanded, dropping pretense. They both knew. That part of her that knew screamed for her to run, to listen to it, but Nevaeh knew better, knew that no matter what choice she made now, nothing would ever be on again but this *off*, this *off* was better. She raised her fingers and sighed.

CONTRIBUTORS

Giuseppe Balestra aka **GB** is a young illustrator based in Italy. He generally works in pen and inks, hatching and stippling, sometime adding digital color. Balestra has provided illustrations for various artistic projects, books, artbooks, comics and posters, both in Europe and in the USA, including *Poster Spy – Alternative Movie Poster Collection* and *Printed in Blood's The Thing: Artbook*.

Trained as an architect, **Paul L. Bates** embraced a career in construction management during a protracted recession in the early 1970s. He is now in the throes of a lengthy—albeit admittedly much underappreciated—writing *career*. He is grateful to Jon Padgett for offering a platform for its expression, and to Thomas Ligotti for providing a source of immeasurable inspiration. Paul is retired, lives on the shore of a small lake in western Massachusetts with his wonderful girlfriend and two very strange cats.

Deborah Bridle currently teaches at the Université de Nice Sophia Antipolis (Université Côte d'Azur) while continuing her research work in British and American literature. Her research focuses on fiction dealing with the fantastic. After defending a doctoral dissertation on the image of the mirror in a selection of Victorian fairy tales, her interests have expanded and are now turned to specific subgenres of the fantastic, such as weird fiction and supernatural horror. She is particularly interested in occultism and mysticism in the works of authors from the end of the nineteenth century like Arthur Machen, as well as in the nihilistic philosophical approaches in the works of twentieth-century writers of horror like H.P. Lovecraft and Thomas Ligotti.

Alana I. Capria is the author of the novel *Mother Walked Into the Lake* and the story collection *Wrapped in Red*. She has an MFA in Creative Writing from Fairleigh Dickinson University. Capria resides in Northern New Jersey with her husband and rabbit. Her website is <u>alanaicapria.com</u>.

Donyae Coles is just trying to survive the America. Stories help. You can follow her on Twitter: @okokno.

C. M. Crockford is a writer on the autistic spectrum. His fiction, poetry and criticism have been published in *The Were-Traveller*, *Neologism Poetry Journal*, *Better Than Starbucks*, *Nasty Women & Bad Hombres*, *Dark Gothic Resurrected*, and *No Recess! Magazine*. He currently lives in Philadelphia, PA.

Tatiana Garmendia's work synthesizes formal concerns and a humanist engagement with history and culture. Born in Cuba at the height of the Cold War and immigrating to the USA as a youth, the artist's practice deciphers myths, histories, languages, and tropes from different communal fonts. This variability is reflected in her use of interdisciplinarity and hybrid narratives reporting on lived experiences, real and imagined. She has exhibited her work throughout the USA and abroad. Her works are in public collections in Seattle, New York, Washington D.C., Miami, Illinois, California, Ohio, and the Dominican Republic.

Robin Gow is a poet, editor, and LGBTQ+ educator. He's recently been published in *POETRY*, *New Delta Review*, and *Into the Void*. His first full-length poetry collection is forthcoming with Tolsun Books and his second is forthcoming with Weasel Press. He is a professor and MFA candidate at Adelphi University and has facilitated LGBTQ+ inclusivity trainings for universities and healthcare networks across the country.

Danielle Hark is a writer and artist who lives with bipolar disorder and PTSD. She's the founder of the non-profit Broken Light Collective that empowers people with mental health challenges using photography. Danielle lives and creates in New Jersey with her husband, two daughters, Samoyed pup, and Scottish Fold cat. www.daniellehark.com / Instagram: @daniellehark.

S. C. Hickman is a Resistance Blogger, poet, storyteller, writer of weird tales, off-beat humorist and comic fatalist. Hickman is also an avid political and social satirist. Last but not least: he is a volunteer clown at the local rodeo. Got to keep them laughing! Hickman is retired, living in the mountains near Yellowstone with his lovely horses, dogs, and partner; not necessarily in that order.

Trent Kollodge has stories in *Autumn Cthulhu* and *Strangely Funny IV*, and a self-published novel, *Two-Bit Angel*. He enjoys time with his family, origami, and the warm weather in Austin, Texas. Someday, he will write again - maybe.

Andrew Koury is a horror writer living in Cincinnati, Ohio. He works in prose, screenwriting, and comics. You can find him online at andrewskoury.wordpress.com or on Twitter at @andrewskoury.

Christi Nogle's short stories have appeared in publications such as *Pseudopod, Nightscript, Escape Pod,* and *Lady Churchill's Rosebud Wristlet.* She teaches college composition and lives in Boise, Idaho with her partner Jim and their dogs and cats. You can follow her at christinogle.com or on Twitter @christinogle.

Valin Paige is a spoken word poet living in St. Paul, Minnesota. She has a spoken word album entitled *Bleed Through* and is published in *Button Poetry* and *Coffin Bell.* She is currently an MFA student at Hamline University.

Eden Royce is from Charleston, South Carolina, now living in the Garden of England. Her short stories are in various print and online publications including *The Year's Best Dark Fantasy & Horror* (2018), *Sycorax's Daughters* (Bram Stoker Award finalist), *Strange Horizons*, and *PseudoPod.* Her debut, middle grade, historical Southern Gothic novel, *Tying the Devil's Shoestrings,* is forthcoming from Walden Pond Press/HarperCollins. Find more at edenroyce.com.

Lucy A. Snyder is the five-time Bram Stoker Award-winning author of over sixty published poems that have appeared in publications such as *Asimov's Science Fiction, Nightmare Magazine,* and *Weirdbook.* Her most recent books are the collection *Garden of Eldritch Delights* and the forthcoming novel *The Girl With the Star-Stained Soul.* She also wrote the collections *While the Black Stars Burn, Soft Apocalypses,* and *Chimeric Machines.* You can learn more about her at www.lucysnyder.com.

D. P. Watt lives between Scotland and England in an otherworldly, misty borderland. His collection of short stories *An Emporium of Automata* was reprinted by Eibonvale Press in early 2013, and his second collection, *The Phantasmagorical Imperative and Other Fabrications*, was published in 2014 with Egaeus Press and is now available in a paperback edition. His third collection *Almost Insentient, Almost Divine was published* in 2016 by Undertow Publications and was nominated for a Shirley Jackson Award. You can find him at The Interlude House: www.theinterludehouse.co.uk.

GRIMSCRIBE PRESS

CPSIA information can be obtained
at www.ICGtesting.com
Printed in the USA
FSHW011523270719
60458FS

9 780578 547275